Great Invention! Now What?

Evaluate, patent, trademark, and license your new invention

D1502950

Great Invention! Now What?

Evaluate, patent, trademark, and license your new invention

Dr. Charles B. McGough, PhD

Self-Counsel Press Inc.
(a subsidiary of)
International Self-Counsel Press Ltd.
USA   Canada

Copyright © 2014 by Self-Counsel Press Inc.

All rights reserved.

No part of this book may be reproduced or transmitted in any form by any means — graphic, electronic, or mechanical — without permission in writing from the publisher, except by a reviewer who may quote brief passages in a review.

Printed in Canada.

First edition: 2014

Library of Congress Control Number: 2014941583

Self-Counsel Press Inc.
(a subsidiary of)
International Self-Counsel Press Ltd.

Bellingham, WA   North Vancouver, BC
USA   Canada

Contents

Samples

Notice to Readers

Laws are constantly changing. Every effort is made to keep this publication as current as possible. However, the author, the publisher, and the vendor of this book make no representations or warranties regarding the outcome or the use to which the information in this book is put and are not assuming any liability for any claims, losses, or damages arising out of the use of this book. The reader should not rely on the author or the publisher of this book for any professional advice. Please be sure that you have the most recent edition.

Note: The fees quoted in this book are correct at the date of publication. However, fees are subject to change without notice. For current fees, please check with the appropriate government office nearest you.

Prices, commissions, fees, and other costs mentioned in the text or shown in samples in this book may not reflect real costs where you live. Inflation and other factors, including geography, can cause the costs you might encounter to be much higher or even much lower than those we show. The dollar amounts shown are simply intended as representative examples.

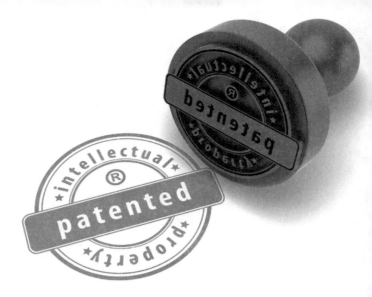

Acknowledgments

I would like to thank my sweetheart, editorial critic, and wife (one and the same person!) for her invaluable assistance in the preparation of this little book. Liz's love of houseplants and travel was the motivation for my first commercial invention. Without her support and dedicated service as "nagger-in-chief," this book would never have been written.

A sincere shout-out to the SCP team — editors, Tanya Lee Howe and Eileen Velthuis; and Publisher and Editor-in-Chief, Kirk LaPointe — for their skillful and patient guidance throughout the publishing process.

CBM
Savannah, GA
June, 2014

1
The Inventor's Yellow Brick Road

This is an exciting time for inventors! On September 16, 2011, the *Leahy-Smith America Invents Act* (AIA) was signed into law. This act marks the first significant change to United States patent law in 60 years. Among its provisions, the new law allocates additional funds to the United States Patent and Trademark Office (USPTO) so it can hire more examiners to reduce its huge backlog of patent applications.

When President Barack Obama signed the bill into law, he said, "Somewhere in that stack of applications could be the next technological breakthrough, the next miracle drug. We should be making it easier and faster to turn new ideas into jobs."[1]

Many Americans today have had at least one great idea for a new product. These ideas are inspired by work, hobbies, recreation, sports, TV, children, travel, medical experiences, or from

---

[1] "Obama signs 1st major patent law change since 1952," *The Colorado Springs Business Journal*, accessed May 27, 2014. http://csbj.com/2011/09/16/obama-signs-1st-major-patent-law-change-since-1952/

simply walking around and observing what people do and need in their everyday lives. Our country has, arguably, the most innovative and creative society in the world. We are a nation of problem solvers, and we solve many problems by inventing exciting new products.

This book was written to help the creative but inexperienced independent inventors who have ideas for new products for consumers and industries. These products may include ideas for new and better tools; board games; manufacturing fixtures; toys, computer games; garden items; athletic equipment; environmental products; hobby aids; apparel; kitchen items; auto accessories, cookware; holiday decorations; medical devices; electronic gadgets; agricultural or farm products; and dozens of other new inventions for work, play, and everyday living.

Although new product ideas will differ greatly, the fundamental steps necessary to evaluate, protect, and market them are quite similar. Depending on the idea, the details will vary in the application of these steps. The sequence and actions, however, will remain basically the same for all.

Many creative people ask: "I have this idea for a great new invention. But now what? How do I turn it into a successful new product?" New inventors are often afraid of explaining their products to others and then having their ideas stolen. These inventors have only a vague understanding of patents and trademarks. They don't know if, when, or how to hire a patent attorney; and they don't have a clue as to how they can successfully market their ideas.

Do not be intimidated. This little book will help you, the new independent inventor, to navigate your way step by step through this scary maze. It is designed to help inventors turn a great idea into a successful commercial product. However, as important as it is to protect an idea with a patent, there are other tasks in this book. The chapters will help you through the complex process of of evaluating your idea, building and testing a working model, obtaining a trademark and patent and finally, finding a good licensee. The book will not force you to wade through a lot of nonessential verbiage, but rather it will help you stay focused like a laser beam on your true objective: To develop and make some money from your great new invention!

This book tells you not just what to do, but also exactly how to do it. It will help to guide you, chapter by chapter, down the inventor's yellow brick road to a successful commercial product. Some of you will make it all the way, while others may simply want the fun and satisfaction of getting the idea patented and trademarked.

Readers of this book will find the steps helpful for pursuing their ideas while minimizing money spent on patent attorneys. Patent attorneys typically charge $200 to $300 per hour, and the cost of having them fully prepare and obtain your patent may cost $5,000 or more.

To work through the chapters in this book, you will require the following:

- Access to a computer with an Internet connection and browser (e.g., Chrome or Explorer) and search engine (e.g., Google), word processing software (e.g., Microsoft Word), and a good printer. You don't have to be a computer expert, but you should be able to use these tools.

- The ability to think and write clearly. This means you should be able to understand straightforward instructions and forms, and write in clear, plain English (not legalese or Pulitzer Prize-quality prose) to describe your idea and how it works.

If either of these requirements exceeds your comfort level, and you don't have someone to help you, consider enrolling in basic computer and business writing courses to improve your skills. After you have the basics, you will find it easier to proceed with this book.

If you're ready, let's begin your independent journey down the inventor's yellow brick road on the way to fame and fortune. Have fun!

2
Who Are These Independent Inventors?

You may be asking yourself the question: "What kind of people are inventors?" The answer is all kinds of people — young, elderly, those with college degrees and those without, retired, working (self-employed or for someone else), men, women, all races and ethnicities, and just about any category of people you can think of. They may have vastly different backgrounds but they all have one thing in common: They recognized a problem or opportunity and they were smart enough to visualize a new invention to solve the problem or meet the opportunity. They are not dreamers or eccentrics or weird — just everyday people who are good observers and problem solvers.

The United States Patent and Trademark Office (USPTO) recently issued its "Performance & Accountability Report" (fiscal year 2013).[1] I don't want to get too deep into the statistical weeds here, but this report contains some very valuable patent

1 "United States Patent and Trademark Office Perfomance & Accountability Report," USPTO, accessed May 27, 2014. www.uspto.gov/about/stratplan/ar/USPTOFY2013PAR.pdf

data which will help independent inventors understand the world of patents better.

In 2013, inventors submitted 563,853 utility patent applications and 177,942 provisional patent applications to the USPTO. In that same year 265,979 utility patents were issued. Obviously, these issued patents all came from applications submitted in previous years. Data from earlier years are quite similar, indicating that about 44 to 47 percent of all utility patent applications actually result in patents. Also, it is interesting to note that 268,719 utility patents which had been issued in earlier years were abandoned in 2013. This is close to the same number (265,979) of new utility patents issued in 2013.

What does all this mean? It means that:

- Every year more than 500,000 individuals and companies believe they have great ideas worth patenting.

- Of the 500,000, about half receive patents.

- Each year, many patents which had been issued in previous years did not prove to be commercially successful and are abandoned, about equal in number to the new patents issued in that same year.

Here's one other fact that should interest you: Of the 265,979 utility patents granted in 2013, 24,084 (9 percent) were issued to independent inventors. These are patents which were not signed over to a company; in other words, the owner is the inventor. For the most part, that's you! The IBMs and GEs of the world do own most of the patents, but there is still room for the average person with a great idea.

Although obtaining a patent is just one of many things that must be done to get your great idea licensed, it is very important. As we say in Logic 101, it is "a necessary but not sufficient condition for success." You must get your idea patented for it to be commercially successful, but even if you do, there are many other critical steps which must be taken.

This book is here to help guide you through the process in the quickest way, for the least amount of your money, and with the greatest chance of success.

Have you ever watched the ABC TV program, *Shark Tank*? This program features ordinary people who have come up with ideas for new products and want to raise money for their start-up businesses. Let's look at a few examples of these clever inventors:

- Two college classmates (one American, one from India) designed a programmable LED lightbulb which can be controlled by an iPhone app to change color, dim, turn on or off, and do other clever things. They applied for a utility patent on their invention and wanted to raise money to start manufacturing the lightbulbs. The problem was that one lightbulb sells for $99! One of the venture capitalists recommended that they not attempt to start a new lightbulb manufacturing enterprise to compete with huge well-established competitors, rather they should try to license it to Philips or another lighting company. Another venture capitalist liked it enough to invest $350,000 in the business! We don't know how this will turn out in the long run but it shows how two smart, young guys with different backgrounds can recognize a need and try to solve it with a clever new invention.

- A young man and wife, both ex-schoolteachers, came up with an idea for a product called Zoobean. They created a computer software package which selects appropriate books for individual children with various needs (e.g. age appropriate, special needs, boys, girls, blended families). For some reason they had not attempted to patent Zoobean. (Maybe they needed this book to help them!) Unfortunately, they were not successful in raising money from the *Shark Tank* venture capitalists.

- A father-and-son team invented a product they called Intelli-Stopper Wine Cork, to be used on open wine bottles to remove air and preserve the life of the wine for up to two weeks. It has a special red band on the stopper which indicates when the wine drinkability is coming to an end. They had submitted a utility patent application, probably a provisional application, for the product.

- A stay-at-home mom in her 30s invented a new toy called Fort Magic. This is a 384-piece kit of plastic tubes and fittings which can be assembled into various toy frames (e.g. forts, cars, tents). Unfortunately the required fabrics were not included, and the kit sold for $199! She didn't raise any money on *Shark Tank*, but she made it to the show and got a huge audience for her invention. This is a good example of a young mother gaining inspiration from her children to design them a new toy!

- Derek Pacque, a recent graduate of Indiana University, had a bad experience with a lost coat-check ticket. This caused him to create a new system, which he called CoatChex, to replace easily lost paper tickets. CoatChex is a mobile collapsible coat check kiosk with special coat hangers in which a customer database of all phone numbers and names replaces the ticket. He's applied for a utility patent on the system, and actually turned down a $200,000 investment by a *Shark Tank* venture capitalist. However, he said the TV show exposure was like a $500,000 infomercial for his invention!

Besides TV shows like *Shark Tank*, news outlets also provide information about inventors and their inventions:

- On April 23, 2014, *USA Today* reported: "A 23-year-old Olympia man who studied mechanical engineering at the University of Washington is finding a market for his invention —lenses that turn your cellphone into a microscope. Thomas Larson's first product is a lens with 15 times magnification, which could be used by coin and stamp collectors, for example."

- A writer named Gayle Jo Carter wrote a short article in *USA Today* a couple of years ago called "Parent Smart: Products Designed by Moms and Dads." She wrote, "When it comes to helpful products for parents, who better to inspire them than moms and dads themselves?" She quoted Janet Chan of *Parenting*, which features parent-inspired products in its magazine, "It's the stuff that comes out of your life that makes you the experts." Carter listed in her article a few of the best parent-designed products:

  - Keep-it-Kleen Pacifier: The pacifier closes instantly when the baby takes it out of his or her mouth or when it is dropped on the floor.

  - Baby Light & Clip: Combines a flashlight and nail clippers to take the guesswork out of cutting the baby's nails.

- Tag Mates™: Cute and easy way to label clothes without sewing or ironing.

- ReliaDose: A dual purpose baby bottle that delivers an accurate dose of liquid medicine to an infant along with a favorite drink.

- Food Cuber: Stackable storage container that holds pre-portioned amounts of food for quick and easy meal preparation.

You may also know people who have invented great products. The following examples are close to home for me:

- My golfing buddy, who is a retired pediatrician, had a poor experience with his wife's surgery. It didn't work out too well for her so he designed a better surgical device to use in back surgery. It takes many years to get a medical device approved and the jury is still out on this one, but it is a good example of where new independent inventors get their ideas.

- Another golfing friend came to me with a device he designed to make it easier to mark an alignment line on his golf ball. Similar products are already on the market. He is still working on his to make improvements.

- A young daughter of a friend travels a lot, staying in youth hostels. She came up with a need for lightweight washable "footsies" (slipper socks) which she could wear in the less-than-sanitary youth hostel showers. It was a good idea but, unfortunately for her, similar products are already on the market.

- A painter working on a friend's house concluded that conventional paint can lids did not work very well. Inspired, he designed a better one which minimizes drips, is easy to open and close, and has many other advantages.

I hope that these examples inspire you to do something big with that great idea you have been sitting on. These people are no smarter than you, and they didn't have this little book to spur them on and guide them through the steps of testing, patenting, trademarking, and licensing their unique ideas!

3
Evaluate Your Idea

It's normal to be excited about a new product idea. If you are not fired up about it and don't want to see it become a real product sold to Walmart, Home Depot, Toys "R" Us, Company XYZ, or wherever, do not proceed further with this book. To do all of the work to make it happen, you can't be lukewarm about your idea. To you, it should be the greatest thing since the proverbial sliced bread!

That said, you have to be realistic when considering whether your idea is truly practical before you invest your time and money into patenting, trademarking, and licensing it.

1. Research Similar Products

If your idea is for a consumer-type product (e.g., toy, tool, game, garden accessory, kitchen appliance, sports item), go to the stores that sell similar products and inspect the items carefully. Ask yourself the following questions and take notes:

- How similar are these products to your idea?

- Does the item essentially do the same thing?

- What do similar products cost?

- Who makes these items?

- Do these products have advantages over your idea?

- What makes your idea better than your competitors' products?

To help you decide if your product is better than what is already on the market, and whether or not to pursue your idea further, continue your research for similar products online so you can learn about the competitors' products. For example, if your idea is for a houseplant-watering device, enter "houseplant waterers" into the search engine; you will be surprised at how many products turn up and how many different companies market those products. You can learn from your competitors' websites how the products work, the pricing of the items, who makes them, and just about anything you want to know about these products. Customer reviews on the websites may also help you to understand the strengths and weaknesses of competing products.

Caution: Don't take all the claims made for any products at face value. They can be exaggerated. If the claims sound suspicious, you should search for other reviews of the product, and buy one and test it yourself.

2. Ask for Feedback

Explain your idea to your trusted friends and relatives. Ask them for their constructive feedback. Be sure to ask your friends to be honest in their critiques. They may want to avoid hurting your feelings, but it is better to find shortcomings earlier in the process rather than later.

Asking others to critique your idea can give you another point of view and help you judge the merits of your idea. These are some of the questions you may want to ask:

- Do you like the product?

- Would you buy one?

- What do you see as the advantages of this product?

- What do you consider the shortcomings of this product?

- What would you be willing to pay for it?

- How often do you think you would use it?

Constructive feedback can save you time and money. For example, one sports-minded inventor came up with the idea of displaying trophy golf balls from famous golf courses around the world by mounting them on a large globe. This would make a very attractive addition to an office or a study. Unfortunately, the idea had some shortcomings. First, simple calculations showed that to mount the desired number of golf balls would require a very large sphere (i.e., globe) which would take up a lot of table or floor space. Second, since some very small countries (e.g., Scotland, Ireland) have dozens of world-class golf courses, the trophy golf balls from these courses would have to be remotely located, which somewhat defeats the purpose of the display. Third, several other products are already on the market which mount trophy golf balls in wall frames. These frames can display hundreds of golf balls without requiring any floor space, and are considerably less expensive than a globe display would be.

3. Be Honest with Yourself

Now, having done your homework, take off the rose-colored glasses and really look at your idea. Ask yourself:

- Will the product work?

- Am I sure that the product can perform the intended function?

- Is there a need or market for the product?

- Will customers buy it?

- Is the idea unique, or are there competing products on the market that do essentially the same thing?

- Will my product be simple to use and maintain? Can it be operated without overly complicated instructions?

- Can the product be manufactured for a reasonable cost?

- Did I receive genuine positive feedback from friends and relatives?

If the answer is "yes" to each of these questions, proceed to Chapter 4. If not, consider revising the idea if it only needs a bit of tweaking. However, if your research isn't going well, maybe you should set it aside for a while to give you some time come up with solutions to its perceived problems. Then, if you are still striking out, you may want to save your resources for another day and move on to your next great idea.

4
Build a Working Model

You may have made some kind of model or sample of your new idea already. If you haven't, now is the time to create one. A working model will be needed to give you confidence that the product can be built and that it will work as intended.

Here's an example of how I created a device for watering houseplants while the owner is away from home. Originally, I came up with the idea in order to alleviate my wife's worries about her many houseplants during an upcoming extended vacation. The idea consisted of a special multilayered disk which would slowly drip water over two to three weeks from a quart plastic bottle into the plant, without becoming clogged from the normal impurities present in all household tap water.

I built 15 to 20 of these devices, using available materials (including a Christmas-light mounting product, pet watering bottles, and laboratory filter paper), and placed them in my wife's houseplants. Upon returning from a month-long trip to Australia, we found the bottles empty and the plants in excellent condition. Eureka!

An invention was born. Much work would be required to develop and commercialize this new idea, as will be shown in the following chapters, but it all started by designing, building, and testing the early handmade models.

Models are not required by the US Patent and Trademark Office in the patent application process. However, models are vital to give you confidence in the idea as well as essential tools for developing, marketing, and licensing your new product.

1. If You Can't Build It, Ask for Help

All independent inventors must find some way to build, or have built, a working model of their new idea. Many new inventors may not have the skills to make their own models. If so, they probably know a friend, relative, local workshop, or other person who could help them carry out this important step.

You may have to pay a workshop to build your model. If you hire the workshop as a form of contractor who builds it to your specifications, the workshop will not be entitled to a share of your invention.

Tip: There are many resources available to aid an imaginative inventor to build a model. The MSC Industrial Supply company catalog (www.mscdirect.com) has close to 5,000 pages of tools, materials, adhesives, fasteners, instruments, machines, lubricants, fluids, piping, tubing, flat stock, electrical devices, and accessories that a model builder may find extremely useful. One independent inventor used more than two dozen items supplied by MSC to build models for several of his inventions.

The Fisher Scientific company catalog (www.fishersci.com) contains thousands of scientific items (e.g., tubing, glassware, measuring instruments) that an inventor can use to build a working model of the new product.

Common office supply catalogs such as those from Office Depot and Staples are gold mines for items that a clever inventor may use to build models. Michael's, Hobby Lobby, and other similar craft and hobby stores may also be good sources for material, depending on the nature of your invention.

Be of good cheer! You were smart enough to come up with your great idea, so building a model will be a piece of cake!

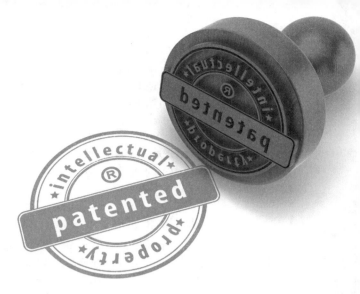

5
Test, Test, Test

As President Ronald Reagan once famously said, "Trust but verify." That's also excellent advice for inventors!

After successfully getting through Chapters 3 and 4, you now trust that you have a unique new product idea which will work as advertised, and that customers are likely to buy and use the product. You must now verify this trust by testing your model. These tests will be crucial in order to convince not only yourself, but everyone with whom you may discuss the idea in the future. Such parties may include the patent examiner, investors, licensees, business partners, or even the legal community if your patent is challenged or infringed upon. This verification testing may take many forms, depending on the nature of your new product.

Returning to the example mentioned in Chapter 4, the house-plant-watering device was tested extensively during the preparation of the patent application, and continued long after the patent was issued. These tests consisted of carefully measuring the rate at which water dripped from the one-quart bottles during a two- to three-week period. The results proved that the special multilayer valve device, called a flo-disk, would release the water at a consistent rate over the desired watering period without becoming clogged from the normal impurities present in all tap water. Many flo-disk design variations were tested during development until the best combination was found, which became the final design ultimately used in production.

1. Record Your Data

It is important to carefully record your test data and other information, such as sketches and photos. This is mainly so you don't forget or get confused about what you have tested, and so you will be able to use this information to convince yourself and future licensees that the product works as advertised.

Data from your tests should be carefully recorded in bound research notebooks. Do not use a loose-leaf binder because pages could get lost or destroyed and such a binder is not as permanent and unalterable as is a bound notebook. Avery or Wilson Jones 12-column account books work well for documenting most of the test data.

Record your test data, notes, and sketches in ink (do not use pencil) and initial and date each page, and have the book signed and dated by a witness when completed.

Please note that the common sense recommendations for recording and preserving your data are not intended to be legal advice as to how to fully protect your invention if it is ever challenged in a courtroom. If you believe that your ownership of your invention may be disputed in the future, you may want to discuss this with a patent attorney who can advise you. A legal challenge is very rare for an amateur inventor and should not be a major concern if you follow the steps described in the book.

2. Test Your Product

After ensuring that the new houseplant-watering device dispensed water at the intended rate without plugging (i.e., one quart over two to three weeks), I ran comparative tests with many houseplants to demonstrate the effectiveness of the device in actual use. I set up ten different plant specimens in pairs, with the watering device in one of the plants but not the other, and photographed the plants over several weeks. The photos showed dramatic differences in the condition of the watered versus unwatered plants, which proved that the new invention worked as intended.

Another example of testing involved an inventor who set out to design a toilet seat lid which would automatically close after use (a guaranteed marriage saver!). The goal was a simple, non-electronic, low-cost lid which could be used in new toilets or retrofit to existing toilets. The product was not intended to compete with the very expensive, high-end automatic toilets already on the market. The gravity-activated design worked in theory; however, the tests showed it to be too bulky and impractical so the idea was dropped.

Because there are many types of new products and devices which independent inventors create, there is no single procedure for testing them. Not all products can be tested like the watering device. However, every new product idea can and must be tested in some way to show that it will work as intended.

If it's a new tool, for example, the development model must be tested under a variety of extreme conditions to show that it will perform as intended and that it is superior to competitive tools. Similarly, models of a new toy or board game should be tested with age-appropriate children to see if they can use it easily and enjoy it. A new piece of athletic gear should be tested by actual athletes to get their feedback, and appropriate measurements taken. A new car accessory (e.g., a child's car seat) must be tested under actual operating conditions. A new biodegradable product for irrigating newly planted reforestation seedlings must be tested, to show that the seedlings with the irrigation device survive better than those without the device under dry planting conditions.

No matter what your new product idea is, build a good model, test it extensively under all expected operating conditions, use the data from the tests to modify and improve the model, and keep good test records (i.e., in ink, bound notebook, signed and witnessed).

Testing should be an ongoing process throughout the life of your invention, and once you have completed the early proof-of-principle tests you will have the confidence in your idea which you need to proceed to the next steps to develop, protect, and market your idea.

Thomas Edison systematically tested hundreds of materials before he came up with one that worked with his incandescent lightbulb. You can surely run a few dozen tests to develop your own great invention!

6
Estimate the Cost of Your New Product

Now that you are convinced your idea is unique and useful, and you have begun testing a working model, it's time to look closely at one of the most important factors which will determine its commercial success: cost.

As the old saying goes, "You can do anything for a price." This means that you can probably have your product manufactured no matter what it is, but at what cost? For your idea to be attractive to potential buyers or licensees, they must be convinced that they can build and sell it at a reasonable profit.

At this point, you do not need to contact manufacturers to ask for quotes to build it, but you should try estimating its manufacturing costs. This preliminary cost estimate will be important in convincing future licensees to take a license from you to build and sell it. As will be explained in Chapter 11, the royalties from this license agreement will be your payment — your ultimate goal after all this work!

1. Calculate the Cost

If your new product is a tool, game, household appliance, fashion accessory, apparel item, or other product which will be sold through retail stores or in catalogs, you should research the price of similar items. Note the prices of similar or competitive products in stores and on the Internet.

Now, working backward, if a competing or similar product is selling for $20 in Home Depot or Lowe's, that item was probably sold to the store by the manufacturer for about $10, which gives the store its desired 50 percent gross profit. Gross profit (as a percentage) is defined as the selling price minus the cost, divided by the selling price, or $(20 - 10)/20 = 0.50$, or 50 percent.

Similarly, the manufacturer must make a profit on the product, typically 50 percent gross profit. Therefore, if the manufacturer sells your product to Home Depot for $10, the manufacturer must be able to make it for about $5 in order to achieve the 50 percent gross profit.

The gross profit targets will vary from item to item and store to store. But if the product manufacturer is not convinced that both the business and the retail customers will be able to achieve reasonable profit margins, the manufacturer will not be willing to take on the risk of making and selling your new product, no matter how great you think it is. Therefore, a good rule of thumb is: The cost of manufacturing your new product should be no more than 20 to 25 percent of its estimated retail selling price.

If your new product requires expensive materials, a highly complex design, difficult manufacturing methods, or other features which raise the manufacturing costs so high that its retail price would be noncompetitive, then the idea will not be commercially attractive to potential licensees or buyers.

The next step is to estimate the manufacturing cost. This will depend on your product and your own estimating skills and experience. If your product does not require exotic materials, expensive electronic components, or unusual manufacturing techniques, and is similar to other reasonably priced products, it may be safe to assume that your own product can be manufactured for a competitive cost and you need not worry further about the cost issue at this time.

However, your idea may be so unique that it does not have obvious competitive products already on the market. If your new product solves an important problem, the manufacturing cost may not be the greatest concern in this early stage of your invention.

In another scenario, you may be an expert in the field and be in an excellent position to prepare a detailed manufacturing cost estimate of your new device. For example, you may be a machinist or an electronic craftsperson who can determine quite accurately what the cost of your new tool or device will be. Having a good manufacturing cost estimate will give you an edge when negotiating with future interested parties.

2. Reduce the Cost of Your Product

The important message of this chapter is that the cost of manufacturing your new product will be a very important factor in determining its commercial success or failure. Gather as much cost information as you can.

If you can determine that your product can probably be built for about 25 percent or less of its estimated retail selling price, excellent. However, if you cannot do that, at least make sure that your invention will not be so difficult and expensive to build, compared to its value to the user, that no profit-minded manufacturer will be interested in it. If you find that this may be the case, work hard to reduce the manufacturing costs by changing materials, simplifying its design, or taking other cost-reduction steps which may be appropriate for your specific invention, before making the investment in time and dollars which will be required to patent and market the product.

7
File Your Provisional Application for Patent

You are now convinced that you have a great idea, and that the idea has real potential for becoming a practical, cost-effective product which people will buy and use. Now is the time to begin protecting the idea by filing what the United States Patent and Trademark Office (USPTO) calls a "Provisional Application for Patent Cover Sheet." The provisional application is a quick, low-cost method of establishing an early legal patent filing date for your invention. This filing date is important because it is the date when your invention officially goes on record with the USPTO. If, at some later time, someone claims to have invented your product, your USPTO provisional application filing date will be critical to establish your rights to the invention.

As noted in the Chapter 2, the US patent laws were significantly revised by the *America Invents Act* in 2011. One of the most important changes to the law was that after March 16, 2013, it allowed granting of a patent based on the "first inventor to file" principle, rather than the "first to invent" principle as was the case under previous patent law. This means that if you file first with the USPTO and obtain a patent, your patent is deemed to take precedence over any later filings by others and you are deemed to be the true inventor. This change was made to make US patent laws consistent with those of other countries, and to reduce the amount of litigation over who actually has the patent rights to a new product.

The new law makes the timely filing of a provisional application even more critical because the provisional application gives the inventor a crucial legal filing date for the invention, (as long as a nonprovisional patent application is filed within 12 months). As will be explained more fully in Chapter 10, the nonprovisional patent application is the true legally binding patent which will give the inventor exclusive right to the invention for 20 years from the date of filing.

1. Complete the Provisional Application for Patent

The Provisional Application for Patent allows you to officially record your invention without many of the elements which will be needed in the important nonprovisional patent application which you will file later (see Chapter 10). For example, the provisional application does not require any formal patent claims, or a disclosure statement about earlier similar inventions, called "prior art," which are required in the nonprovisional application.

The patent office does not examine the provisional application as it does a nonprovisional application. However, your description of the invention should be as complete as possible in the provisional application so that it can support the nonprovisional application when it is filed.

Filing the provisional application gives the inventor 12 months in which to file the nonprovisional application. Note that this period cannot be extended and you cannot resubmit the same application. If the nonprovisional application is not filed before the 12-month period expires, the filing date afforded by the provisional application will be lost.

You cannot add any new technical information to your nonprovisional application which was not included in the provisional application description. If you do add new information, you will lose the benefit of the early provisional application filing date. You can, however, submit an entirely new provisional application with the new information, but it will be given its own new filing date.

The Provisional Application for Patent Cover Sheet (form PTO/SB/16) will be included in the inventor's package mailed to you by the USPTO Contact Center (see section **2.**). You can also use the blank form that is included in the download kit (see the Download Kit page at the end of this book). Remember, all ideas are different and you must make sure that your provisional application describes your idea clearly, and in the format required by the USPTO. See Sample 1, located at the end of this chapter for more information on how to complete the provisional application.

You must submit a Specification (a written description of the invention), and the drawings that are necessary to understand it, with the Provisional Application for Patent Cover Sheet as shown in Sample 2. If you have some talent for drawing, or an engineering background, you can prepare the drawings yourself. If not, you may want to have someone do this for you, although it's not necessary to hire a draftsperson or other professional to prepare these informal drawings.

The USPTO defines a small independent inventor as a "micro entity" if the person's maximum qualifying gross income, as defined by the Internal Revenue Service, does not exceed three times the median US household income. As of January 2014 that amount is $153,051. Many readers of this book will probably qualify as micro entities, which you will do by completing the Certification of Micro Entity Status (form PTO/SB/15A) as shown in Sample 3. If you do not qualify as a micro entity, you will be classified as a "small entity" and your fees will almost double.

Along with the Provisional Application for Patent, Specification, and Micro Entity Status, you'll need to submit the filing fee for an independent inventor. The fee at the time of this book's printing was $65 for a micro entity.

In summary, the following includes the most important things to remember about the provisional application:

- It is a simple filing method with a low fee which quickly gets your invention a filing date on record with the USPTO.

- It gives you one year to assess the invention's commercial potential before you have to commit to the higher cost of filing a nonprovisional application.

- It gives you the right to use the notice "patent pending" for one year.

- It allows you to begin immediate promotion of the invention with greater security against having it stolen.

- It does *not* allow you to add any new technical material into the nonprovisional application that was not included in the provisional application description.

The provisional application is a great asset to the small inventor, so prepare it as soon as possible. When completed, mail the forms and application fee to the following address:

Commissioner for Patents
PO Box 1450
Alexandria, VA 22313-1450

Tip: Use a large US Postal Service Priority Mail envelope and include a self-addressed, stamped postcard with your important information on it (i.e., name of invention, your name, the form number). The USPTO will date and stamp it and mail it back to you as a quick confirmation of receipt.

Good work! You have now passed a critical mile marker on the independent inventor's road to success!

2. Available Resources

The US Patent and Trademark Office (USPTO) publishes a brochure entitled "Provisional Application for Patent" which gives you clear and concise instructions on how to prepare and submit your application. To obtain the most recent edition of this brochure, call the USPTO Contact Center (telephone: 1-800-786-9199, dial 2 for patents and 5 to speak to a customer service representative). Ask the representative to mail you the independent inventor's package. It will contain the "Provisional Application for Patent" brochure and several other very useful booklets.

Another valuable resource is the Inventor's Assistance Center (www.uspto.gov/inventors/iac/index.jsp or 1-800-786-9199).

The customer representatives will assist you with completing forms, answer your questions about fees and regulations, and direct you to the right person to answer further questions, if necessary. This office can be very helpful as you proceed through the patent and trademark process.

Sample 1
PROVISIONAL APPLICATION FOR PATENT

PTO/SB/16 (03-13)
Approved for use through 01/31/2014. OMB 0651-0032
U.S. Patent and Trademark Office; U.S. DEPARTMENT OF COMMERCE
Under the Paperwork Reduction Act of 1995 no persons are required to respond to a collection of information unless it displays a valid OMB control number

PROVISIONAL APPLICATION FOR PATENT COVER SHEET – Page 1 of 2
This is a request for filing a PROVISIONAL APPLICATION FOR PATENT under 37 CFR 1.53(c).

Express Mail Label No. _____

INVENTOR(S)

Given Name (first and middle [if any])	Family Name or Surname	Residence (City and either State or Foreign Country)
John	Smith	Bakersfield, California

Additional inventors are being named on the _____ separately numbered sheets attached hereto.

TITLE OF THE INVENTION (500 characters max):

Biodegradable Device for Irrigating Seedlings and Other Small Plants

Direct all correspondence to: **CORRESPONDENCE ADDRESS**

[ ] The address corresponding to Customer Number:

OR

[✓] Firm or Individual Name John Smith

Address **123 1st Avenue**

City Bakersfield	State California	Zip 12345
Country United States	Telephone 555-555-5555	Email email@email.com

ENCLOSED APPLICATION PARTS (*check all that apply*)

[ ] Application Data Sheet. See 37 CFR 1.76.   [ ] CD(s), Number of CDs _____

[✓] Drawing(s) *Number of Sheets* 2 _____   [ ] Other (specify) _____

[✓] Specification (e.g., description of the invention) *Number of Pages* 2 _____

Fees Due: Filing Fee of $260 ($130 for small entity) ($65 for micro entity). If the specification and drawings exceed 100 sheets of paper, an application size fee is also due, which is $400 ($200 for small entity) ($100 for micro entity) for each additional 50 sheets or fraction thereof. See 35 U.S.C. 41(a)(1)(G) and 37 CFR 1.16(s).

METHOD OF PAYMENT OF THE FILING FEE AND APPLICATION SIZE FEE FOR THIS PROVISIONAL APPLICATION FOR PATENT

[ ] Applicant asserts small entity status. See 37 CFR 1.27.

[✓] Applicant certifies micro entity status. See 37 CFR 1.29.
Applicant must attach form PTO/SB/15A or B or equivalent.

[✓] A check or money order made payable to the *Director of the United States Patent and Trademark Office* is enclosed to cover the filing fee and application size fee (if applicable).

$65.00

TOTAL FEE AMOUNT ($)

[ ] Payment by credit card. Form PTO-2038 is attached.

[ ] The Director is hereby authorized to charge the filing fee and application size fee (if applicable) or credit any overpayment to Deposit Account Number: _____

USE ONLY FOR FILING A PROVISIONAL APPLICATION FOR PATENT
This collection of information is required by 37 CFR 1.51. The information is required to obtain or retain a benefit by the public which is to file (and by the USPTO to process) an application. Confidentiality is governed by 35 U.S.C. 122 and 37 CFR 1.11 and 1.14. This collection is estimated to take 10 hours to complete, including gathering, preparing, and submitting the completed application form to the USPTO. Time will vary depending upon the individual case. Any comments on the amount of time you require to complete this form and/or suggestions for reducing this burden, should be sent to the Chief Information Officer, U.S. Patent and Trademark Office, U.S. Department of Commerce, P.O. Box 1450, Alexandria, VA 22313-1450. DO NOT SEND FEES OR COMPLETED FORMS TO THIS ADDRESS. **SEND TO: Commissioner for Patents, P.O. Box 1450, Alexandria, VA 22313-1450.**
If you need assistance in completing the form, call 1-800-PTO-9199 and select option 2.

Sample 1 — Continued

PTO/SB/16 (03-13)
Approved for use through 01/31/2014. OMB 0651-0032
U.S. Patent and Trademark Office; U.S. DEPARTMENT OF COMMERCE
Under the Paperwork Reduction Act of 1995 no persons are required to respond to a collection of information unless it displays a valid OMB control number

PROVISIONAL APPLICATION FOR PATENT COVER SHEET – Page 2 of 2

The invention was made by an agency of the United States Government or under a contract with an agency of the United States Government.

[✓] No.

[ ] Yes, the invention was made by an agency of the U.S. Government. The U.S. Government agency name is: _____

[ ] Yes, the invention was made under a contract with an agency of the U.S. Government. The name of the U.S. Government agency and Government contract number are: _____

WARNING:

Petitioner/applicant is cautioned to avoid submitting personal information in documents filed in a patent application that may contribute to identity theft. Personal information such as social security numbers, bank account numbers, or credit card numbers (other than a check or credit card authorization form PTO-2038 submitted for payment purposes) is never required by the USPTO to support a petition or an application. If this type of personal information is included in documents submitted to the USPTO, petitioners/applicants should consider redacting such personal information from the documents before submitting them to the USPTO. Petitioner/applicant is advised that the record of a patent application is available to the public after publication of the application (unless a non-publication request in compliance with 37 CFR 1.213(a) is made in the application) or issuance of a patent. Furthermore, the record from an abandoned application may also be available to the public if the application is referenced in a published application or an issued patent (see 37 CFR 1.14). Checks and credit card authorization forms PTO-2038 submitted for payment purposes are not retained in the application file and therefore are not publicly available.

SIGNATURE John Smith _____ DATE August 1, 20-- _____

TYPED OR PRINTED NAME John Smith _____ REGISTRATION NO. Leave Blank _____
(*if appropriate*)

TELEPHONE 555-555-5555 _____ DOCKET NUMBER Leave Blank _____

SPECIFICATION (PROVISIONAL PATENT APPLICATION)

BIODEGRADABLE DEVICE FOR IRRIGATING SEEDLINGS AND OTHER SMALL PLANTS

Inventor: Charles B. McGough

BACKGROUND OF THE INVENTION

Technical Field
This invention pertains to the field of plant husbandry (Class 047)*

*Note: The USPTO classifies all inventions using a classification code system. This class number is used to direct nonprovisional patent applications to the appropriate department (e.g., art unit) for examination. There are literally thousands of class codes and subcodes to describe everything under the sun. You can research the USPTO website to try to find the exact code that best fits your invention; however, the simplest and quickest way for the first-time inventor to find a code is to look at the patents of other similar products and use the same code number. You can search Google Patents, as is explained in Chapter 8. If the class number is not quite right for your invention, the examiner will change it. No big deal and certainly not worth the effort to learn the arcane patent-coding system unless you are studying to become a patent attorney or agent!

Description of Prior Art
US Patent 5,896,700, *Device for Watering Unattended Houseplants* (Charles B. McGough, Inventor), describes a device which dispenses a quantity of water (typically 16 or 32 ounces) to a potted houseplant over an extended period of time (typically 1 to 2 weeks or more) without owner intervention. The device is completely passive, operates by gravity flow, uses standard tap water, and solves a number of problems not addressed by earlier houseplant watering devices.

The -700 device is comprised of three major components: (1) a reservoir consisting of a plastic bottle with top-filling opening and a threaded lower exit neck; (2) a base assembly consisting of a matching threaded cap and a narrow tapered spike which supports the reservoir and provides an open path for passage of water into the plant root region; (3) a disk-shaped sandwich-type wafer constructed of several layers of gasket material, laboratory filter paper, and thin plastic, having through-holes and passages so constructed to filter impurities from the water and control the rate at which water is released from the reservoir during the desired watering period.

The major advantages of the -700 device includes: it reliably and efficiently dispenses the reservoir water over a specified period; it releases its water at a relatively uniform rate during the watering cycle; it uses standard tap water; its performance is not affected by ambient or soil conditions; it is simple to install and operate; and it is inexpensive to manufacture.

The -700 device has been on the market for several years and has proven to be an effective method for watering a wide variety of unattended houseplants.

SUMMARY OF THE INVENTION

The device disclosed in this Provisional Application is a modification and new application of the invention covered by US Patent 5,897,700 described in the previous section. This biodegradable one-time-use device is designed to provide water to newly planted reforestation seedlings and other such plantings to prevent them from drying out in the critical period after planting. The device is comprised of two components: (1) a unique version of the flow-control wafer described in the -700 patent, herein called a drip-control disk; and (2) a biodegradable plastic bag capable of holding 1 gallon (typically) of water, having a reclosable top opening for filling the water, and into which is permanently installed in the drip-control disk. After the bag is filled with water it is placed near the base of the newly planted seedling or plant, with the drip-control disk downward, where it will slowly release its water over a specified time period (typically 2 to 3 weeks) to keep the plant roots moist. After the bag empties it will slowly degrade into the soil so as to not leave debris in the forest or planting area.

BRIEF DESCRIPTION OF THE DRAWINGS

Figure 1 is an overall view of the device showing the biodegradable plastic bag with reclosable top-fill port and the drip-control disk near the bottom.

Figure 2 shows details of the drip-control disk installed in the biodegradable plastic bag. The disk is placed in a hole in the bottom of the bag, with its drip hole facing outward. The hole in the bag is approximately the same diameter as the disk. A larger diameter thin plastic circle, with a center hole somewhat larger than the drip hole in the disk, and having an adhesive on its top surface, is placed over the outside of the bag and disk to seal the disk firmly to the bag. The water from the bag, acting under the influence of its static pressure, then enters the side of the filter paper and flows toward the center where it drips slowly through the drip hole into the soil.

An alternate method of sealing the drip-control disk to the bag is to design the bag with a hole somewhat smaller in diameter than the disk, place the disk against the inside surface of the bag, and bond the bag and lower plastic layer of the disk together using a heat-seal process.

Figure 3 illustrates the method of controlling the drip rate through the disk. During manufacture a hard ring somewhat greater in diameter than the drip hole is compressed against the top surface of the disk. This drives the adhesive on the surfaces of the two plastic layers into the filter paper creating a restriction in the path which the water must take to exit through the drip hole. The amount of compression determines the drip rate. For example, a light compression during manufacture will result in a fast drip rate, and a greater compression will slow the drip rate, so that the desired time to empty the water in the bag can be achieved. This principle is similar to that described in the -700 patent.

DESCRIPTION OF PREFERRED EMBODIMENT

A device for irrigating seedlings and other plantings, especially immediately after planting, to ensure that the roots of said plantings remain moist, consists of a biodegradable plastic bag with a typical capacity of 1 gallon of water, said bag having a reclosable top opening and, at the bottom, a multilayered disk which regulates the rate at which water is slowly released from the bag. In the preferred embodiment the reclosable top opening is a zipper-type design which will enable the person who plants the seedling to quickly fill, close, and place the bag by the plant. Other non-zipper type closures may also be used. The drip-control wafer will release the contents of the bag over the desired period, typically 1 gallon over 2 to 3 weeks. Alternatively, other capacities and release times may be used, depending on the specific needs of the plant. The preferred method of attaching the drip-rate disk to the bag is by heat sealing the plastic surface, but the alternate method using a separate adhesive-surface plastic disk (see Figure 2) is also acceptable.

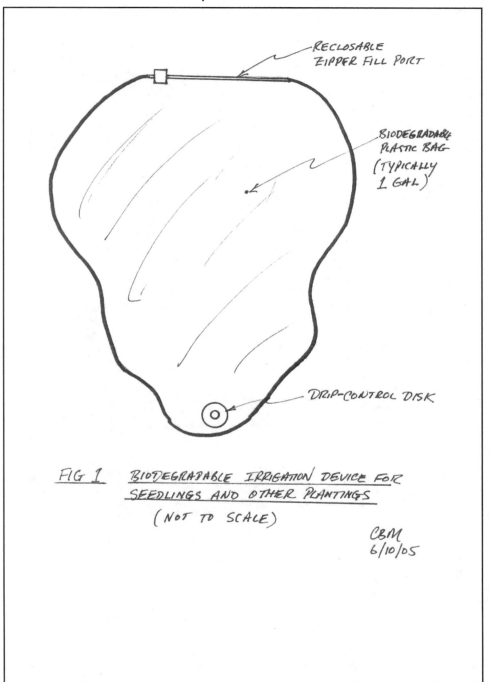

RECLOSABLE
ZIPPER FILL PORT

BIODEGRADABLE
PLASTIC BAG
(TYPICALLY
1 GAL)

DRIP-CONTROL DISK

FIG 1   BIODEGRADABLE IRRIGATION DEVICE FOR
SEEDLINGS AND OTHER PLANTINGS
(NOT TO SCALE)

CBM
6/10/05

Sample 2 — Continued

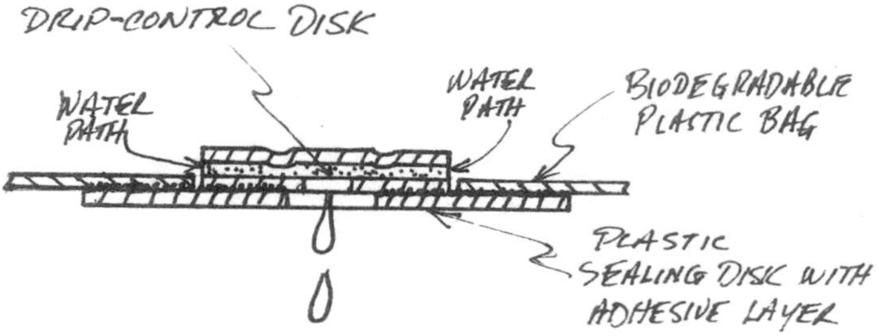
DRIP-CONTROL DISK
WATER PATH
WATER PATH
BIODEGRADABLE PLASTIC BAG
PLASTIC SEALING DISK WITH ADHESIVE LAYER

FIG 2 DRIP-CONTROL DISK INSTALLED IN BIODEGRADABLE PLASTIC BAG
(NOT TO SCALE)

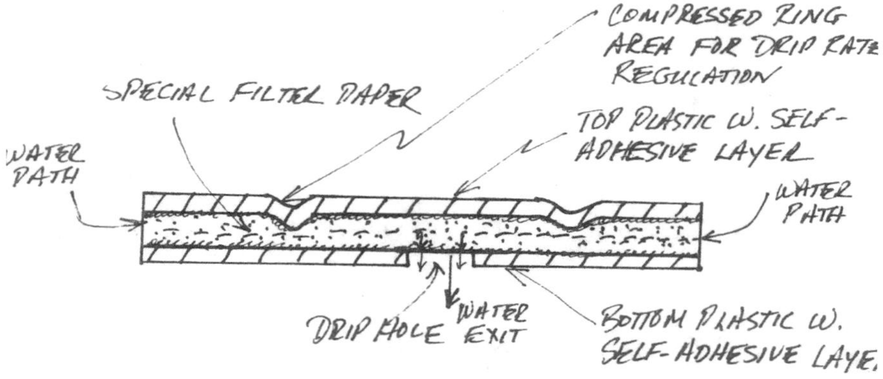
COMPRESSED RING AREA FOR DRIP RATE REGULATION
SPECIAL FILTER PAPER
TOP PLASTIC W. SELF-ADHESIVE LAYER
WATER PATH
WATER PATH
DRIP HOLE
WATER EXIT
BOTTOM PLASTIC W. SELF-ADHESIVE LAYE.

FIG 3 DRIP-CONTROL DISK
(NOT TO SCALE)

CBM
6/10/05

Sample 3
CERTIFICATION OF MICRO ENTITY STATUS

Doc Code: MES.GIB
Document Description: Certification of Micro Entity Status (Gross Income Basis)

PTO/SB/15A (03-13)

CERTIFICATION OF MICRO ENTITY STATUS
(GROSS INCOME BASIS)

Application Number or Control Number (if applicable):	Patent Number (if applicable):
Leave Blank	Leave Blank

First Named Inventor:	Title of Invention:
John Smith	Biodegradable Device for Irrigating Seedlings and Other Small Plants

The applicant hereby certifies the following—

(1) **SMALL ENTITY REQUIREMENT** - The applicant qualifies as a small entity as defined in 37 CFR 1.27.

(2) **APPLICATION FILING LIMIT** - Neither the applicant nor the inventor nor a joint inventor has been named as the inventor or a joint inventor on more than four previously filed U.S. patent applications, excluding provisional applications and international applications under the Patent Cooperation Treaty (PCT) for which the basic national fee under 37 CFR 1.492(a) was not paid, and also excluding patent applications for which the applicant has assigned all ownership rights or is obligated to assign all ownership rights as a result of the applicant's previous employment.

(3) **GROSS INCOME LIMIT ON APPLICANTS AND INVENTORS** - Neither the applicant nor the inventor nor a joint inventor, in the calendar year preceding the calendar year in which the applicable fee is being paid, had a gross income, as defined in section 61(a) of the Internal Revenue Code of 1986 (26 U.S.C. 61(a)), exceeding the "Maximum Qualifying Gross Income" reported on the USPTO website at http://www.uspto.gov/patents/law/micro_entity.jsp which is equal to three times the median household income for that preceding calendar year, as most recently reported by the Bureau of the Census.

(4) **GROSS INCOME LIMIT ON PARTIES WITH AN "OWNERSHIP INTEREST"** - Neither the applicant nor the inventor nor a joint inventor has assigned, granted, or conveyed, nor is under an obligation by contract or law to assign, grant, or convey, a license or other ownership interest in the application concerned to an entity that, in the calendar year preceding the calendar year in which the applicable fee is being paid, had a gross income, as defined in section 61(a) of the Internal Revenue Code of 1986, exceeding the "Maximum Qualifying Gross Income" reported on the USPTO website at http://www.uspto.gov/patents/law/micro_entity.jsp which is equal to three times the median household income for that preceding calendar year, as most recently reported by the Bureau of the Census.

SIGNATURE by a party set forth in 37 CFR 1.33(b)

Signature	John Smith				
Name	John Smith				
Date	August 1, 20--	Telephone	555-555-5555	Registration No.	

☐ There is more than one inventor and I am one of the inventors who are jointly identified as the applicant. Additional certification form(s) signed by the other joint inventor(s) are included with this form.

8
Name Your Product and Apply for a Trademark

You've now passed the halfway mark by making it to Chapter 8! It's time to have some fun by creating a unique name for your product. To give your product's name extra protection, you may want to consider trademarking the name. This chapter will help you discover a great name for your product as well as how to trademark it.

1. Create a Great Name for Your Product

Every new product needs a good name. A catchy, descriptive name will help you sell your idea to prospective licensees and, eventually, to the end users of your product. Of course, even a great name cannot make up for a poor product. However, if you have followed all of the other instructions, as discussed in the previous chapters, a good name will improve your chances of success.

Now consider the names of popular products and how well known they have become over the years:

- Hula Hoop
- Tervis Tumbler
- Frisbee
- Jitterbug
- Silly Putty
- BreatheRight
- Slinky
- 7UP
- Topsy-Turvy
- Sharpie
- Uni-ball
- Kleenex
- Swiffer
- Gatorade
- Titleist
- Post-it
- Snapple
- Bic
- Krazy Glue
- Coca-Cola

We could list hundreds of names which identify successful products that have become well known to the buying public. Here are some more examples from new patented and patent-pending product names by an independent inventor:

- *Plantastic!:* A smart houseplant-watering system for vacationing plant owners.

- *EasyPrime:* A tool for priming hard-to-start swimming pool pumps.

- *Seedling Soaker:* A biodegradable bag system with a slow-release component for keeping fragile reforestation tree seedlings moist.

- *Treesaver:* An improved plastic bag system which releases water over five days to small or newly planted trees.

Try to think of a short, simple name for your product which you can use in correspondence, but don't spend too much time or money on this. Your future licensee will have his or her own ideas and may rename it. As an example of this, my houseplant-watering product was called by its trademarked name *Plantastic!* when it was built and sold by its first licensee. When a new licensee took over, he renamed the same product the *Jobe's Smart Watering System* to take advantage of his well-known name and brand in garden products. I said, "Great! Whatever it takes to sell more of them."

If you are having trouble coming up with a good, catchy name, you may want to ask others for help in naming your product. There are many companies and consultants who specialize in finding names for products, and companies on the Internet which advertise that they will help you find a good name for your product, but these services will cost you money. At this point, I believe hiring someone for help is overkill. Simply talk to your friends and family and come up with a short (preferably one word), cool (but not too cool) name that is easy to remember, say, and spell, and which will give the reader a clue to the nature of your product. If you're really desperate for ideas, Google "product naming" to see what others have done.

2. Trademark the Name of Your Product

If you do come up with a unique, catchy name for your product you may want to trademark it. A trademark registration is easier to acquire and less expensive than a patent; however, it provides protection only for the name, not the product itself. The latter, obviously, is far more important.

The US Patent and Trademark Office (USPTO) defines a trademark as "a word phrase, symbol, and/or design that identifies and distinguishes the source of the goods of one party from those of others (www.uspto.gov/trademarks/basics/definitions.jsp, accessed May 27, 2014)."

You can receive a trademark registration by filing an application to register your product name with the USPTO stating that you have a bona fide intention to use the trademark in commerce.

Before you file for a trademark, you would be wise to conduct a search to see if the name is already registered. To do this, go to www.trademarkia.com and enter your proposed name in the search box. The website will tell you if anyone has registered that name, how many registrations there are, and the status of each. For example, the name "Plantastic" has been registered five times, although only "Plantastic!" is currently active and the other four marks have expired. "EasyPrime" and" SeedlingSoaker" have no registered trademarks; and "Treesaver" has been registered five times and one mark is currently active.

If you find that your proposed name has no active registered trademarks you can proceed with confidence that you will be able to register it. The simplest way is to pay a trademark company to do it. For example, Trademarkia will do this for you for $159 plus the cost of the filing fee (price current at the time of this book's publication). I recommend this approach only if you are uncomfortable filing yourself.

Again, you can use the helpful services provided by the USPTO for small inventors and call 1-800-786-9199 (press 1 for trademark information and 5 to speak to a representative). Ask the representative to mail you the inventor's trademark package. This package will include a very useful brochure called "Basic Facts about Trademarks," which will walk you through the process and give you instructions for filing. You can also find the brochure online (see the Resources file in the download kit for a link to this brochure).

You will be using the Trademark Electronic Application System (TEAS) to register your product name. Although you could file a paper application, the USPTO strongly prefers that you file electronically, which has many advantages such as a lower application fee, quicker response time, and a review of your application to help you avoid errors.

You can find the application and the instructions by going to www.uspto.gov/trademarks/teas/index.jsp. Complete the application as directed. The form is very self-explanatory and gives you helpful information, including fee payment instructions. The TEAS online filing fee is currently $325. Fees may change annually, so be sure to check with the USPTO website for the current fee schedule. Sample 4 is an example of a trademark Certificate of Registration.

You can also use TEAS PLUS which has additional requirements. TEAS PLUS has a $50 lower application fee but it requires a lot more work; for example, selecting an entry from the USPTO's Acceptable Identification of Goods and Services manual (see the Resources file in the download kit for a link to this brochure). I think that you will have more important work to do so I recommend you pay the extra $50 and use TEAS.

Once you claim your right to a trademark you may begin using the symbol ™ in your advertising and correspondence. After the USPTO registers your trademark, you may use the symbol.

The term of your registration is ten years, so every ten years you'll need to renew your trademark name. USPTO recommends starting the renewal process a year before your trademark expires. Trademark registrations can be renewed indefinitely and good ones may be quite valuable, as the owners of the Gatorade name can testify.

You are now ready to let the rest of the world know about your great idea!

TRADEMARK CERTIFICATE OF REGISTRATION

The United States of America

CERTIFICATE OF REGISTRATION
PRINCIPAL REGISTER

The Mark shown in this certificate has been registered in the United States Patent and Trademark Office to the named registrant.

The records of the United States Patent and Trademark Office show that an application for registration of the Mark shown in this Certificate was filed in the Office; that the application was examined and determined to be in compliance with the requirements of the law and with the regulations prescribed by the Director of the United States Patent and Trademark Office; and that the Applicant is entitled to registration of the Mark under the Trademark Act of 1946, as Amended.

A copy of the Mark and pertinent data from the application are part of this certificate.

This registration shall remain in force for TEN (10) years, unless terminated earlier as provided by law, and subject to compliance with the provisions of Section 8 of the Trademark Act of 1946, as Amended.

Director of the United States Patent and Trademark Office

Requirements for Maintaining a Federal Trademark Registration

SECTION 8: AFFIDAVIT OF CONTINUED USE

The registration shall remain in force for 10 years, except that the registration shall be canceled for failure to file an Affidavit of Continued Use under Section 8 of the *Trademark Act*, 15 U.S.C. §1058, upon the expiration of the following time periods:

i)   At the end of 6 years following the date of registration.
ii)   At the end of each successive 10-year period following the date of registration.

Failure to file a proper Section 8 Affidavit at the appropriate time will result in the cancellation of the registration.

SECTION 9: APPLICATION FOR RENEWAL

The registration shall remain in force for 10 years, subject to the provisions of Section 8, except that the registration shall expire for failure to file an Application for Renewal under Section 9 of the *Trademark Act*, 15 U.S.C. §1059, at the end of each successive 10-year period following the date of registration.

Failure to file a proper Application for Renewal at the appropriate time will result in the expiration of the registration.

No further notice or reminder of these requirements will be sent to the Registrant by the Patent and Trademark Office. It is recommended that the Registrant contact the Patent and Trademark Office approximately one year before the expiration of the time periods shown above to determine the requirements and fees for the filings required to maintain the registration.

Int. Cl.: 21
Prior U.S. Cls.: 2, 13, 23, 29, 30, 33, 40, and 50

Reg. No. 2,421,619
United States Patent and Trademark Office   **Registered Jan. 16, 2001**

TRADEMARK
PRINCIPAL REGISTER

PLANTASTIC!

MCGOUGH, CHARLES B. (UNITED STATES CITIZEN)
123 Main Street
Any Town, Any State 55555
8-12-2000

IN CLASS 21 (U.S. CLS. 2, 13, 23, 29, 30, 33, 40 AND 50).
FIRST USE 2-0-1998; IN COMMERCE

FOR: CONTAINERS FOR HOLDING WATER WHICH ARE PLACED ON SOIL IN A POT AND WHICH SLOWLY RELEASE WATER TO PLANTS.

SN 75-183,020, FILED 10-17-1996.

BILL DAWE, EXAMINING ATTORNEY

9
Identify Your Market and Find a Licensee

By now you will be brimming with confidence! Your product works, you have tested it, it has important advantages over competing products, it can be made at a reasonable cost, and it has a great trademarked name. You have protected it by filing your provisional application and you now have 12 months to find a licensee for it before you have to take the big step of preparing and filing your nonprovisional application.

You have two options at this point:

1. You can set up your own company to manufacture and sell the product.

2. You can find an experienced company already making similar products and license your new product to it. This company, called the "licensee," will make it, sell it, and pay you a royalty for each unit sold.

Unless you already have your own company and the new product can be added to an existing product line, I strongly recommend that you pursue the second option and attempt to find a good licensee.

Setting up your own company involves many issues beyond the scope of this book, and if you are determined to do this, there are many business books on the market which can help you. Therefore, this chapter focuses on the task of identifying your market and finding a good licensee for your product.

1. Identify the Market for Your Product

You may already be familiar with the market for your product. For example, if you are a machinist and have an idea for a better tool, you already know the main tool manufacturers who might be interested in your idea. Similarly, if you are a musician with a new music product, or an athlete with an idea for a new sports accessory, or a fisherman with an idea for a better reel, you probably know the names of the major manufacturing companies in those fields.

In that case you should Google those companies and find their websites. Then, from the websites find the names of the right people to contact (e.g., President, VP Sales and Marketing, VP Business Development). Call the company and tell them that you would like to send a letter to the appropriate person about your new product. Some of the large companies have specific procedures that must be followed before they will review any new product ideas. If so, follow the procedures carefully when submitting your product.

2. Send a Proposal Letter to Potential Licensees

Once you have the name and address of the best person in the company to receive your proposal letter, your next step is to write a good proposal letter to that person explaining, in no more than two pages, what your product is, why it is beneficial, and include any other important information (e.g., drawings, photos) that will pique the person's interest.

The proposal letter is critical since it is the principal tool for finding a company willing to license, manufacture, and sell your product.

Your proposal letter (see Sample 5) should:

- Provide a short but descriptive subject line that states the name of your product and what it is.

- Use a strong opening sentence that summarizes who you are and who will buy your product, and that it has a patent pending.*

- Explain the rationale for the product in the body of the letter; namely what problem the product solves, the customer need it satisfies, how it is better than competing products, how it can save the buyer money, and similar topics appropriate to the nature of your product.

- Explain in more detail how your product works by including photos, sketches, and drawings, as needed.

- Summarize your estimate of the cost of manufacturing the product.

- Estimate the size of the market and how many units can be reasonably expected to be sold in the US annually. By using the Internet, you may be able to research this, depending on your product.

- State what you are looking for, namely an established company in the field to manufacture and sell the product under an exclusive license agreement.

- Offer to send samples and to visit the company to demonstrate the product.

- Thank the reader for reviewing your proposal and ask him or her to call or email you to discuss it.

- Include your contact information (i.e., phone number and email address).

*Note: In your letter, state that you have a patent pending on the device, but do not say, at this time, that it is a Provisional Application for Patent. Do not use the number assigned to the provisional application by the US Patent and Trademark Office (USPTO). Some larger companies will not even look at your invention unless it is patented. If the company is interested in the idea, there will be plenty of time later to get into more detail regarding the patent application. As your discussions progress, you will, of course, have to reveal that your patent application is provisional. By this time you will probably have your nonprovisional patent application underway (see Chapter 10) which will supersede the provisional application when filed with the USPTO.

I must emphasize the importance of this proposal letter, and urge you to give it your best shot. Have it reviewed by others and revise it as necessary until you are convinced that it is as good as it can get.

After you're satisfied the proposal letter is ready to be sent, mail copies of identical letters to the appropriate contact officer in as many different companies as you can find that fit your product's market. Do not mail only one letter and sit back and wait for a reply. Mail them all at the same time. Use USPS priority mail flat-pack envelopes for maximum impact, and to help distinguish your letter from the addressee's other correspondence.

Make a list of all the people to whom you have sent the proposal letter. If you do not hear from them within three weeks, follow up with a phone call or an email. You may have trouble reaching the right person. Be persistent but polite when talking with the people you contact.

Once you have generated interest in your product from a potential licensee, have given the responding company all of the data and information it asks for, have possibly met with someone in the company, and you judge that there is a truly interested person or company, you can begin preparing to file your nonprovisional patent application and thinking about the terms of a license agreement, as described in Chapters 10 and 11.

PROPOSAL LETTER

August 1, 20--

Mr. John Doe
President

PoolMagic, Inc.
7000 Swimming Pool Lane
Sacramento, CA 94000

Subject: *EASYPRIME** A tool for priming air-locked swimming pool pumps

Dear Mr. Doe:

I am the inventor and owner of a simple but effective new patent-pending tool designed to be used by those who service and/or own in-ground swimming pools.

As you know, swimming pool pumps can be difficult to start because of air lock, which can occur when the system is opened up for normal servicing or repair. For many reasons including, for example, an aging pump, a small air leak in the system, or the pump being elevated too high above the pool, the "self-priming" feature does not always work and the pump does not automatically begin to pump the pool water as intended. Instead, it may run for long periods (15 to 20 minutes or longer) without priming itself and pumping the pool water properly. This is not only annoying and time consuming to the pool-service person, but it also risks overheating and damaging the pump motor. When air locking occurs, the pool-service person must open the pump strainer pot, pour four to five gallons of water into the system, and quickly try to restart the pump. This often requires several attempts, which may or may not be successful, and is heavy and time-consuming work for the pool-service person.

I have designed a simple tool called *EASYPRIME**, which completely eliminates the need for this laborious procedure by enabling a quick, nonlabor intensive, guaranteed method, whereby an unassisted pool-service person can quickly restart an air-locked pool pump on the first attempt.

The three attached photos are self-explanatory, showing the *EASYPRIME** tool made from four standard components, attached to a garden hose, and inserted into a surface skimmer pot. The product is very easy to use. If the pool pump is turned on and fails to self-prime, *EASYPRIME** is attached to a garden hose and inserted into one of the pool's skimmer pots as shown. The water from *EASYPRIME** then fills the line, drives out entrapped air, and allows the pump to quickly prime itself.

EASYPRIME* can be a great time and money saver for professional pool-service companies, and also would be a valuable tool for the 5 to 6 million US pool owners, many of whom service their own pools.

It can be made very inexpensively in China (approximately $2 per tool), and if retailed in the US for $15, would generate very acceptable profit margins for the manufacturer. I think that it is not unrealistic to expect to reach 1 percent of the market (50,000 pieces per year) within the first year after launch.

I am seeking an established pool equipment company to manufacture and sell this product to pool-service professionals and pool owners in the US. I believe that PoolMagic, Inc., with its extensive line of quality swimming pool accessories, would be an excellent company to do this.

If you think that this product would make a successful complement to the PoolMagic, Inc. line, I would be pleased to send you a sample and to discuss with you how we could proceed to make *EASYPRIME** a profitable new product for both our companies. My experience is that an exclusive license agreement would work best for this new product.

Please call or email me to discuss. Thank you.

Sincerely,

John Smith

John Smith
email@email.com
555-555-5555

Attachment
*Patent pending

10
File Your Nonprovisional Patent Application

If you have come this far, it is clear that you remain determined to license and sell your product. The time has now come to file for, and eventually receive, a US patent to protect your idea. Until you have a patent issued, or at least a nonprovisional patent application pending, manufacturers will not be interested in talking to you. No company is willing to risk the substantial start-up investment required to launch a new product which, if successful, could be copied and sold by others.

Filing your application for a nonprovisional patent is a big deal, and will be the most important and expensive part of converting your great idea into a successful commercial product. For that reason you should have a licensee in place, or you should at least have generated enough interest in your product that you are confident you will be able to sign up a good company to license, build, and sell your product, before you commit to the work and expense of filing for your nonprovisional patent.

If you have not reached this point, you may want to defer the nonprovisional patent application. Remember, the 12-month clock is ticking on your Provisional Application for Patent. If you do not want to see the benefit of the provisional application exclusivity protection expire, you must file your nonprovisional application within this 12-month window.

According to the US Patent and Trademark Office (USPTO), "A patent is an intellectual property right granted by the Government of the United States of America to an inventor 'to exclude others from making, using, offering for sale, or selling the invention throughout the United States or importing the invention into the United States' for a limited time in exchange for public disclosure of the invention when the patent is granted (www.uspto.gov/patents, accessed May 27, 2014)." For example, if a foreign company copied your idea and sold it to the ABC retail store chain, both ABC and the foreign manufacturer could be sued by you and face substantial penalties. No reputable US seller would knowingly do this. Having the patent in place will give your potential licensee/manufacturer confidence that it will have the exclusivity it needs to proceed.

The term of the patent is 20 years from the date of filing. However, if you file the nonprovisional application near the end of the 12-month exclusivity period given to you by the provisional application (see Chapter 7), you will have almost 21 years in which you can prevent others from selling a knock-off of your product in the US. After the patent period expires you will lose your exclusive protection. You cannot reapply for the same invention but you may continue to make and sell your product.

As mentioned in Chapter 7, the USPTO Contact Center is an indispensable source of information for the independent inventor. From the inventor's package you requested and received you should now review the booklet "General Information Concerning Patents," if you have not already done so. The booklet notes, for example, that the patent law states that any person "who invents or discovers any new and useful process, machine, manufacture, or composition of matter, or any new and useful improvement thereof, may obtain a patent." This definition encompasses practically all products made and the processes used to make them. You can find a link to the booklet in the Resources file in this book's download kit.

It is important to emphasize that an inventor cannot patent an idea; it has to be a physical product based on the idea. You must provide a good description of the actual product and include drawings in your patent application.

Your invention must be new and not obvious to anyone skilled in its field. In other words, it cannot receive a patent if it was known or used by others in the US, patented in a foreign country, or described by others in a printed publication before the date of your invention. The invention also can't be so simple that anyone who understands the industry could know how to do it. For example, purple jeans would not be patentable.

Note that as the inventor, you must file your nonprovisional patent application within one year of using the invention in public, describing it in a printed publication, or offering it for sale. If you do not meet this deadline, you will not be issued a patent.

1. Apply for a Nonprovisional Utility Patent

The nonprovisional utility patent includes machines, processes, manufactured articles, chemical compounds, and much more. The utility category will cover essentially all of your great ideas. The majority of the 400,000 applications received annually by the US Patent and Trademark Office (USPTO) are for utility patents.

The other two types of nonprovisional patent applications are the design patent and the plant patent. Plant patents cover such things as hybrid seeds and newly grafted plant species. The design patent is for new fabric patterns and other such artistic items.

1.1 Conduct a patent search

If you are confident that your product will satisfy the basic requirements of a utility patent, your next step is to conduct a preliminary patent search to see if anyone has already patented your idea.

Google Patents is a valuable tool which makes it easy for you to do a search. It enables you to search the entire body of 8 million patents and 3 million patent applications. All of this information comes from the USPTO and is in the public domain. Google has converted this huge database into a format that makes it easy for the amateur inventor to search for free.

Type "Google Patents" into your search engine and when the site loads, type in your patent category. The search will list patents and patent applications in this patent category, ranked according to Google's opinion of relevance to the category.

Review the drawings and abstract of the first patent listed. If it is similar to your invention, print the information for future use. If it isn't similar, click the next patent listed. Repeat this process until you have reviewed all patents and applications in your patent category.

After completing this preliminary search, you will have a good idea whether someone has beaten you to the punch and patented your idea. If that is the case, you will have to either abandon the idea or make substantive changes to it so you will not infringe on the existing patent.

You should also be aware that when you file your nonprovisional application, the patent examiner will conduct a more thorough search which will include publications and foreign patents, and he or she may reject your claim based on what is found during that search.

If you are confident that your idea is unpatented, original, useful, and nonobvious, then you should continue the process of applying for your nonprovisional patent.

1.2 Elements of the nonprovisional application

Preparing, filing, and negotiating a nonprovisional application is a complex undertaking and you shouldn't attempt it without legal assistance. This advice is even more relevant since the *America Invents Act* became law. Only a trained patent attorney or patent agent will be familiar with the procedural requirements of the new act. (See section **2.** for information on how to find a patent agent or attorney.) You can save money by doing some parts of the application before hiring a patent attorney or an agent.

The mandatory elements of your utility patent application will consist of the following (samples are included at the end of this chapter):

1. Utility Patent Application Transmittal: PTO/AIA/15 (see Sample 6).

2. Fee Transmittal Form: PTO/SB/17 (see Sample 7).

3. Declaration for Utility or Design Patent Application: PTO/AIA/08 (see Sample 8).

4. Specification (see section **1.3** and Sample 9):

   • Title of invention.

   • Cross-reference to related applications.

   • Statement regarding any federally sponsored research or development.

   • Background of the invention.

   • Summary of the invention.

   • Brief description of the drawings.

   • Detailed description of the invention.

   • Claims.

   • Abstract.

5. Drawings (see section **1.4** and Sample 10).

You can prepare a draft of all these elements before contacting a patent attorney or a patent agent, except for the section in the specification under claims (see Sample 9). As the inventor, you know your invention better than anyone, and the information provided in the specification and the drawings you prepare will be necessary to enable the patent attorney or agent to clearly understand your invention. Your attorney or agent will probably revise the specification section and arrange to have the final drawings prepared according to the specific USPTO requirements.

The other three elements (see Samples 6, 7, and 8) in the application process are basically administrative forms. You can complete these forms yourself by following the samples provided at the end of this chapter or you could ask the patent attorney or agent to complete them.

1.3 Specification

As you will see, the specification has many components. Refer to Sample 9 as you read through the following bullet list.

- **Title of invention:** The title of the invention should be short, specific, and unambiguous.

- **Cross-reference to related applications:** You will need to insert this statement: "This application claims priority to, and the benefits of, US Provisional Patent Application Serial Number_(insert serial number)____, filed on (month, day, year)."

- **Statement regarding federally sponsored research and development:** If you have received a government grant for the invention, you will fill in those details here. If you haven't received a grant, state "not applicable."

- **Reference to sequence listing, a table, or a computer program listing compact disc appendix:** This section refers to material submitted separately on a compact disc. The USPTO accepts computer program listings, gene sequence listings, and tables of information on CD. For most new inventors, this section will not apply so you can write "not applicable."

- **Background of the invention:** In the field of endeavor section you will need to include this statement: "This invention pertains to the field of _____(Class number) _____." You can obtain the class number by looking at the classes of several of the similar prior art patents, or by getting a classification listing from the USPTO website and choosing the best fit.

   As the inventor, you have an obligation to reveal to the USPTO any information of which you are aware that could be important to the examiner. To do this you should summarize the most relevant patents which you discovered in your Google Patent Search (see section **1.1**), called the "prior art." You should briefly note how your invention differs from each prior art invention; for example, what problems your product solves that the others do not. If you are aware of any publications that discuss your invention, you must list these also.

- **Summary of the invention:** Before you complete this section, you should complete the detailed description of the invention. When you have completed that section, it will be easier to do the summary of the invention. State briefly the substance, general concept, and purpose of your invention. Note its advantages, the problems it solves (if applicable), and the unique features compared to other similar ideas.

- **Brief description of the drawings:** You should include at least one drawing in your patent application. List all drawings by number (e.g., Figure 1a, Figure 1b; Figure 1, Figure 2) and briefly state what each drawing describes.

- **Detailed description of the invention:** This is where you describe what your invention is and how it works. As the inventor, you know more about your invention than anyone. You should describe it as completely and clearly as you can. Explain how your invention is different from, and better than, other inventions.

  Your invention may be a machine, process, or manufactured article, but you must describe it so that anyone "skilled in the art" can understand it. You must also explain, if applicable, your best mode for carrying out the invention (called the "preferred embodiment"). You should also discuss in detail each element of every drawing.

  Your version of the description may be good enough to go directly into the application. More likely, it will help your patent attorney or agent understand the invention so he or she can rewrite this section, if necessary, for clarity and compliance with USPTO regulations. Be as complete as possible in describing your invention. It will be easier for your attorney or agent to edit and shorten your draft, if necessary, than to add new material that only you know.

- **Claims:** The claims will be the heart of your patent. This section explicitly and concisely defines what you believe to be the essence of the invention. Most important, the claims define the scope of the invention's protection in case your patent is legally challenged or you have to take legal steps to prevent someone from infringing on it in the future. Note that your utility patent application must have at least one claim.

Because the claim section is so critical to gain approval of the application by the USPTO examiner, and will be the basis of any legal actions which may arise in the future, this section should be completed by a patent attorney or agent. For those reasons I strongly advise you to hire an experienced patent attorney or patent agent to draft the claims section of the specification and, if he or she believes it to be necessary, conduct a more comprehensive prior art search.

- **Abstract:** The abstract will allow readers to quickly understand the general nature of your patent. It will be very useful to those who are conducting patent searches, as you undoubtedly found when you conducted your own Google Patent search, and anyone who wishes to learn about your patent. The abstract should clearly summarize your description and claims in narrative form (no drawings), in a single paragraph of 150 words or less.

1.4 Drawings

Utility patents should have at least one drawing. The drawings are necessary to enable a reviewer to understand the invention and how it works. They must show all of the features described in the claims section.

Drawings are normally in black ink and on white paper; color drawings and photographs are rarely permitted and require special approval by the USPTO. The USPTO has very specific and unbending specifications for patent drawings. The drawing requirements are defined by Title 37 of the Code of Federal Regulations, specifically 37CFR.1.84. To appreciate their complexity and detail, please refer to "A Guide to Filing a Utility Patent Application," and "General Information Concerning Patents." Links to both of these can be found in the Resources file in this book's download kit or, if you have the inventor's package, they are included in it.

Because of the complexity and specificity of the USPTO drawing requirements, your final version of the drawings should be done by a professional drafting firm with experience preparing patent drawings. Your patent attorney or agent can help you find a good firm to do this.

The USPTO does allow you to submit your utility patent application with clear, understandable, black and white drawings, but which do not necessarily meet all the 37CFR 1.84 requirements. If there is a problem, the examiner will send your patent attorney an "Office Action" stating that the drawings do not meet the standards. The Office Action may list other items that must be addressed, most commonly some other prior art references that you will have to rebut. It is extremely rare for a utility patent application to sail through to acceptance without at least one Office Action.

This approach allows you to defer the expense of having the drawings prepared by a draftsperson until you are confident that you will be able to clear all of the examiner's objections and have your patent issued.

When you have written the first draft of the specification (without claims) and made your drawings, your patent attorney or agent will be in a good position to complete and file the application. His or her main tasks for filing will be to revise or rewrite your specification, write (with your participation) the claims, and complete the declaration and two transmittal forms.

The declaration (see Sample 8) is simply a notarized statement by you that you and no one else is the original inventor of the subject matter. The application (see Sample 6) and fee transmittal (see Sample 7) forms are essentially self-explanatory.

1.5 Filing fees

At the time of this book's publication the fees you, as a micro entity, will be required to pay with the application are a $70 electronic filing fee, a $150 utility search fee, and a $180 examination fee, totaling $400. When the patent is approved, you will pay a $240 issue fee. These fees are subject to change annually, often in October. Your attorney or agent will advise you on this.

2. Find a Patent Attorney or Patent Agent

It is not recommended that you attempt to prepare your patent application completely on your own. It has been done successfully in the past by non-lawyers, including the author of this book, but it takes special skills and experience that most new inventors do not possess. A good patent attorney or patent agent is essential for preparation of the application, especially the claims section, and to guide the application through the complicated and arcane negotiation process with the USPTO examiner.

The special forms, terminology, procedures, requirements, and filing dates are too difficult for the average novice inventor to learn. As noted in section **1.4**, your application will most probably be rejected the first time it is submitted in a document from the examiner called an Office Action. This will require the filing of an Amendment. Many of these initial rejections come when the examiner uncovers publications or foreign patents that were not considered in the application. Your attorney or agent will guide you through the Office Actions and Amendments maze until, hopefully, your application satisfies the examiner, is approved, and your patent is issued.

How do you find a patent attorney or patent agent? Here again the USPTO website can help you (see the Resources file in the download kit for a link to registered patent attorneys and agents). You will find a complete listing of more than 10,000 patent agents and 31,000 patent attorneys who are registered with the patent office. These patent attorneys and patent agents (non-attorneys with patent experience) are all registered and qualified to practice with the USPTO. Non-registered attorneys or agents are not approved to deal with the USPTO and cannot help you. The huge lists of registered attorneys and agents are, fortunately, organized by state, so you should have no problem finding several people in your area.

After you select a few candidate agents or attorneys, arrange meetings where you can show each one your invention and all of the work you have done to prepare the application. Ask them to give you a firm not-to-exceed price for completing, filing, and negotiating the application through the USPTO until the patent issues or is finally rejected.

If the attorney or agent believes your idea is patentable, he or she may be willing to discount his or her normal fee because of all the work you have already done. Talk to several attorneys and agents, and then make your selection based on reputation, how you feel about them, and their fees.

Congratulations! You have now completed one of the most important parts, the filing of a nonprovisional patent application to protect your great new idea. That's good news!

Now the bad news: The patent office is severely understaffed and has a backlog of more than 700,000 unreviewed applications. It takes an average of three years for a patent to be issued. But take heart, the previously discussed *America Invents Act* has provided the USPTO with a bigger budget so it can hire more examiners. This will reduce the approval time and make it easier and faster to turn new ideas into patents.

Once issued, your patent will give you 20 years of exclusivity in the US from the date of filing. With your application now officially in the pipeline you can continue with confidence to line up and license a qualified company to make and sell your great new product.

Sample 6
UTILITY PATENT APPLICATION TRANSMITTAL
(NONPROVISIONAL APPLICATION)

PTO/AIA/15 (03-13)
Approved for use through 01/31/2014. OMB 0651-0032
U.S. Patent and Trademark Office; U.S. DEPARTMENT OF COMMERCE
Under the Paperwork Reduction Act of 1995 no persons are required to respond to a collection of information unless it displays a valid OMB control number

UTILITY PATENT APPLICATION TRANSMITTAL
(Only for new nonprovisional applications under 37 CFR 1.53(b))

Attorney Docket No.	Leave blank
First Named Inventor	John Smith
Title	Biodegradable Device for Irrigating Seedlings and Other Small Plants
Express Mail Label No.	Leave blank

APPLICATION ELEMENTS
See MPEP chapter 600 concerning utility patent application contents.

ADDRESS TO:
Commissioner for Patents
P.O. Box 1450
Alexandria, VA 22313-1450

1. [✓] **Fee Transmittal Form** (PTO/SB/17 or equivalent)
2. [ ] **Applicant asserts small entity status.** See 37 CFR 1.27
3. [✓] **Applicant certifies micro entity status.** See 37 CFR 1.29. Applicant must attach form PTO/SB/15A or B or equivalent.
4. [✓] **Specification** [Total Pages 11] Both the claims and abstract must start on a new page. (See MPEP § 608.01(a) for information on the preferred arrangement)
5. [✓] **Drawing(s)** (35 U.S.C. 113) [Total Sheets 2]
6. **Inventor's Oath or Declaration** [Total Pages ____] (including substitute statements under 37 CFR 1.64 and assignments serving as an oath or declaration under 37 CFR 1.63(e))
   - a. [✓] Newly executed (original or copy)
   - b. [ ] A copy from a prior application (37 CFR 1.63(d))
7. [ ] **Application Data Sheet** * See note below. See 37 CFR 1.76 (PTO/AIA/14 or equivalent)
8. **CD-ROM or CD-R** in duplicate, large table, or Computer Program (Appendix)
   - [ ] Landscape Table on CD
9. **Nucleotide and/or Amino Acid Sequence Submission** (if applicable, items a. – c. are required)
   - a. [ ] Computer Readable Form (CRF)
   - b. [ ] Specification Sequence Listing on:
     - i. [ ] CD-ROM or CD-R (2 copies); or
     - ii. [ ] Paper
   - c. [ ] Statements verifying identity of above copies

ACCOMPANYING APPLICATION PAPERS

10. [ ] **Assignment Papers** (cover sheet & document(s)) Name of Assignee _____
11. [ ] **37 CFR 3.73(c) Statement** (when there is an assignee)   [ ] **Power of Attorney**
12. [ ] **English Translation Document** (if applicable)
13. [ ] **Information Disclosure Statement** (PTO/SB/08 or PTO-1449)
    - [ ] Copies of citations attached
14. [ ] **Preliminary Amendment**
15. [✓] **Return Receipt Postcard** (MPEP § 503) (Should be specifically itemized)
16. [ ] **Certified Copy of Priority Document(s)** (if foreign priority is claimed)
17. [ ] **Nonpublication Request** Under 35 U.S.C. 122(b)(2)(B)(i). Applicant must attach form PTO/SB/35 or equivalent.
18. [ ] **Other:** _____
    _____
    _____
    _____
    _____

*Note: (1) Benefit claims under 37 CFR 1.78 and foreign priority claims under 1.55 **must** be included in an Application Data Sheet (ADS).
(2) For applications filed under 35 U.S.C. 111, the application must contain an ADS specifying the applicant if the applicant is an assignee, person to whom the inventor is under an obligation to assign, or person who otherwise shows sufficient proprietary interest in the matter. See 37 CFR 1.46(b).

19. CORRESPONDENCE ADDRESS

[ ] The address associated with Customer Number: _____   **OR** [✓] Correspondence address below

Name	John Smith				
Address	123 1st Avenue				
City	Bakersfield	State	California	Zip Code	12345
Country	United States	Telephone	555-555-5555	Email	email@email.com

Signature	John Smith	Date	August 1, 20--
Name (Print/Type)	John Smith	Registration No. (Attorney/Agent)	Leave blank

This collection of information is required by 37 CFR 1.53(b). The information is required to obtain or retain a benefit by the public which is to file (and by the USPTO to process) an application. Confidentiality is governed by 35 U.S.C. 122 and 37 CFR 1.11 and 1.14. This collection is estimated to take 12 minutes to complete, including gathering, preparing, and submitting the completed application form to the USPTO. Time will vary depending upon the individual case. Any comments on the amount of time you require to complete this form and/or suggestions for reducing this burden, should be sent to the Chief Information Officer, U.S. Patent and Trademark Office, U.S. Department of Commerce, P.O. Box 1450, Alexandria, VA 22313-1450. DO NOT SEND FEES OR COMPLETED FORMS TO THIS ADDRESS. **SEND TO: Commissioner for Patents, P.O. Box 1450, Alexandria, VA 22313-1450.**
If you need assistance in completing the form, call 1-800-PTO-9199 and select option 2.

Sample 7
FEE TRANSMITTAL

PTO/SB/17 (03-13)
Approved for use through 01/31/2014. OMB 0651-0032
U.S. Patent and Trademark Office; U.S. DEPARTMENT OF COMMERCE
Under the Paperwork Reduction Act of 1995 no persons are required to respond to a collection of information unless it displays a valid OMB control number

FEE TRANSMITTAL

Complete if known	
Application Number	Leave blank
Filing Date	Leave blank
First Named Inventor	John Smith
Examiner Name	Leave blank
Art Unit	Leave blank
Practitioner Docket No.	Leave blank

[ ] Applicant asserts small entity status. See 37 CFR 1.27.

[✓] Applicant certifies micro entity status. See 37 CFR 1.29.
Form PTO/SB/15A or B or equivalent must either be enclosed or have been submitted previously.

TOTAL AMOUNT OF PAYMENT ($) 400.00

METHOD OF PAYMENT (check all that apply)

[✓] Check [ ] Credit Card [ ] Money Order [ ] None [ ] Other (please identify): _____

[ ] Deposit Account Deposit Account Number: _____ Deposit Account Name: _____

For the above-identified deposit account, the Director is hereby authorized to (check all that apply):

[ ] Charge fee(s) indicated below

[ ] Charge fee(s) indicated below, **except for the filing fee**

[ ] Charge any additional fee(s) or underpayment of fee(s) under 37 CFR 1.16 and 1.17

[ ] Credit any overpayment of fee(s)

WARNING: Information on this form may become public. Credit card information should not be included on this form. Provide credit card information and authorization on PTO-2038.

FEE CALCULATION

1. BASIC FILING, SEARCH, AND EXAMINATION FEES (U = undiscounted fee; S = small entity fee; M = micro entity fee)

Application Type	FILING FEES U ($)	S ($)	M ($)	SEARCH FEES U ($)	S ($)	M ($)	EXAMINATION FEES U ($)	S ($)	M ($)	Fees Paid ($)
Utility	280	140*	70	600	300	150	720	360	180	$400.00
Design	180	90	45	120	60	30	460	230	115	
Plant	180	90	45	380	190	95	580	290	145	
Reissue	280	140	70	600	300	150	2,160	1,080	540	
Provisional	260	130	65	0	0	0	0	0	0	

* The $140 small entity status filing fee for a utility application is further reduced to $70 for a small entity status applicant who files the application via EFS-Web.

2. EXCESS CLAIM FEES

Fee Description	Undiscounted Fee ($)	Small Entity Fee ($)	Micro Entity Fee ($)
Each claim over 20 (including Reissues)	80	40	20
Each independent claim over 3 (including Reissues)	420	210	105
Multiple dependent claims	780	390	195

Total Claims _____ -20 or HP = _____ **Extra Claims** x _____ **Fee ($)** = _____ **Fee Paid ($)** _____
HP = highest number of total claims paid for, if greater than 20.

Multiple Dependent Claims Fee ($) _____ Fee Paid ($) _____

Indep. Claims _____ -3 or HP = _____ **Extra Claims** x _____ **Fee ($)** = _____ **Fee Paid ($)** _____
HP = highest number of independent claims paid for, if greater than 3.

3. APPLICATION SIZE FEE

If the specification and drawings exceed 100 sheets of paper (excluding electronically filed sequence or computer listings under 37 CFR 1.52(e)), the application size fee due is $400 ($200 for small entity) ($100 for micro entity) for each additional 50 sheets or fraction thereof. See 35 U.S.C. 41(a)(1)(G) and 37 CFR 1.16(s).

Total Sheets _____ - 100 = **Extra Sheets** _____ / 50 = **Number of each additional 50 or fraction thereof** _____ (round **up** to a whole number) x **Fee ($)** _____ = **Fee Paid ($)** _____

4. OTHER FEE(S)

Fees Paid ($)

Non-English specification, $130 fee (no small or micro entity discount) _____

Non-electronic filing fee under 37 CFR 1.16(t) for a utility application, $400 fee ($200 small or micro entity) _____

Other (e.g., late filing surcharge): _____ _____

SUBMITTED BY

Signature	John Smith	Registration No. (Attorney/Agent) Leave blank	Telephone 555-555-5555
Name (Print/Type)	John Smith		Date August 1, 20--

This collection of information is required by 37 CFR 1.136. The information is required to obtain or retain a benefit by the public which is to file (and by the USPTO to process) an application. Confidentiality is governed by 35 U.S.C. 122 and 37 CFR 1.14. This collection is estimated to take 30 minutes to complete, including gathering, preparing, and submitting the completed application form to the USPTO. Time will vary depending upon the individual case. Any comments on the amount of time you require to complete this form and/or suggestions for reducing this burden, should be sent to the Chief Information Officer, U.S. Patent and Trademark Office, U.S. Department of Commerce, P.O. Box 1450, Alexandria, VA 22313-1450. DO NOT SEND FEES OR COMPLETED FORMS TO THIS ADDRESS. **SEND TO: Commissioner for Patents, P.O. Box 1450, Alexandria, VA 22313-1450.**
If you need assistance in completing the form, call 1-800-PTO-9199 and select option 2.

Sample 8
DECLARATION FOR UTILITY OR DESIGN PATENT APPLICATION

Doc Code: Oath
Document Description: Oath or declaration filed

PTO/AIA/08 (06-12)
Approved for use through 01/31/2014. OMB 0651-0032
U.S. Patent and Trademark Office; U.S. DEPARTMENT OF COMMERCE
Under the Paperwork Reduction Act of 1995, no persons are required to respond to a collection of information unless it contains a valid OMB control number.

DECLARATION FOR UTILITY OR DESIGN PATENT APPLICATION (37 CFR 1.63)		Attorney Docket Number	Leave blank
		First Named Inventor	John Smith
		COMPLETE IF KNOWN	
		Application Number	Leave blank
■ Declaration Submitted With Initial Filing **OR** ☐ Declaration Submitted After Initial Filing (surcharge (37 CFR 1.16(f)) required)		Filing Date	Leave blank
		Art Unit	Leave blank
		Examiner Name	Leave blank

Biodegradable Device for Irrigating Seedlings and Other Small Plants

(Title of the Invention)

As a below named inventor, I hereby declare that:

This declaration is directed to:

■ The attached application,

OR

☐ United States Application Number or PCT International application number _____

   filed on _____ .

The above-identified application was made or authorized to be made by me.

I believe I am the original inventor or an original joint inventor of a claimed invention in the application.

I hereby acknowledge that any willful false statement made in this declaration is punishable under 18 U.S.C. 1001 by fine or imprisonment of not more than five (5) years, or both.

Authorization To Permit Access To Application by Participating Office

☐ If checked, the undersigned hereby grants the USPTO authority to provide the European Patent Office (EPO), the Japan Patent Office (JPO), the Korean Intellectual Property Office (KIPO), the World Intellectual Property Office (WIPO), and any other intellectual property offices in which a foreign application claiming priority to the above-identified patent application is filed access to the above-identified patent application. See 37 CFR 1.14(c) and (h). This box should not be checked if the applicant does not wish the EPO, JPO, KIPO, WIPO, or other intellectual property office in which a foreign application claiming priority to the above-identified patent application is filed to have access to the above-identified patent application.

In accordance with 37 CFR 1.14(h)(3), access will be provided to a copy of the above-identified patent application with respect to: 1) the above-identified patent application-as-filed; 2) any foreign application to which the above-identified patent application claims priority under 35 U.S.C. 119(a)-(d) if a copy of the foreign application that satisfies the certified copy requirement of 37 CFR 1.55 has been filed in the above-identified patent application; and 3) any U.S. application-as-filed from which benefit is sought in the above-identified patent application.

In accordance with 37 CFR 1.14(c), access may be provided to information concerning the date of filing the Authorization to Permit Access to Application by Participating Offices.

[Page 1 of 2]

This collection of information is required by 35 U.S.C. 115 and 37 CFR 1.63. The information is required to obtain or retain a benefit by the public which is to file (and by the USPTO to process) an application. Confidentiality is governed by 35 U.S.C. 122 and 37 CFR 1.11 and 1.14. This collection is estimated to take 21 minutes to complete, including gathering, preparing, and submitting the completed application form to the USPTO. Time will vary depending upon the individual case. Any comments on the amount of time you require to complete this form and/or suggestions for reducing this burden, should be sent to the Chief Information Officer, U.S. Patent and Trademark Office, U.S. Department of Commerce, P.O. Box 1450, Alexandria, VA 22313-1450. DO NOT SEND FEES OR COMPLETED FORMS TO THIS ADDRESS. **SEND TO: Commissioner for Patents, P.O. Box 1450, Alexandria, VA 22313-1450.**

If you need assistance in completing the form, call 1-800-PTO-9199 and select option 2.

Sample 8 — Continued

PTO/AIA/08 (06-12)
Approved for use through 01/31/2014. OMB 0651-0032
U.S. Patent and Trademark Office; U.S. DEPARTMENT OF COMMERCE
Under the Paperwork Reduction Act of 1995, no persons are required to respond to a collection of information unless it contains a valid OMB control number.

DECLARATION — Utility or Design Patent Application

Direct all correspondence to:	☐ The address associated with Customer Number:		OR	■ Correspondence address below

Name
John Smith

Address
123 1st Avenue

City	State	Zip
Bakersfield	California	12345

Country	Telephone	Email
United States	555-555-5555	email@email.com

WARNING:

Petitioner/applicant is cautioned to avoid submitting personal information in documents filed in a patent application that may contribute to identity theft. Personal information such as social security numbers, bank account numbers, or credit card numbers (other than a check or credit card authorization form PTO-2038 submitted for payment purposes) is never required by the USPTO to support a petition or an application. If this type of personal information is included in documents submitted to the USPTO, petitioners/applicants should consider redacting such personal information from the documents before submitting them to the USPTO. Petitioner/applicant is advised that the record of a patent application is available to the public after publication of the application (unless a non-publication request in compliance with 37 CFR 1.213(a) is made in the application) or issuance of a patent. Furthermore, the record from an abandoned application may also be available to the public if the application is referenced in a published application or an issued patent (see 37 CFR 1.14). Checks and credit card authorization forms PTO-2038 submitted for payment purposes are not retained in the application file and therefore are not publicly available. Petitioner/applicant is advised that documents which form the record of a patent application (such as the PTO/SB/01) are placed into the Privacy Act system of records DEPARTMENT OF COMMERCE, COMMERCE-PAT-7, System name: *Patent Application Files* . Documents not retained in an application file (such as the PTO-2038) are placed into the Privacy Act system of COMMERCE/PAT-TM-10, System name: *Deposit Accounts and Electronic Funds Transfer Profiles* .

LEGAL NAME OF SOLE OR FIRST INVENTOR:
(*E.g.,* Given Name (first and middle (if any)) and Family Name or Surname)
John Smith

Inventor's Signature	Date (Optional)
John Smith	August 1, 20--

Residence: City	State	Country
Bakersfield	California	United States

Mailing Address
123 1st Avenue

City	State	Zip	Country
Bakersfield	California	12345	United States

☐ Additional inventors are being named on the supplemental sheet(s) PTO/AIA/10 attached hereto

[Page 2 of 2]

SPECIFICATION (NONPROVISIONAL PATENT APPLICATION)

TITLE OF INVENTION
Biodegradable Device for Irrigating Seedlings and Other Small Plants

CROSS-REFERENCE TO RELATED APPLICATIONS
(0001) This application claims priority to, and the benefits of, US Provisional Patent Application Serial Number 60/690,723 filed on June 16, 2005.

STATEMENT REGARDING FEDERALLY SPONSORED RESEARCH OR DEVELOPMENT
(0002) Not applicable

REFERENCE TO SEQUENCE LISTING, A TABLE, OR A COMPUTER PROGRAM LISTING COMPACT DISC APPENDIX
(0003) Not applicable

BACKGROUND OF THE INVENTION

1. Field of Endeavor
(0004) This invention pertains to the field of plant husbandry (Class 047), specifically to the irrigation of the newly planted tree seedlings and other small plants.

2. Prior Art
(0005) US Patent 5,896,700 *Device for Watering Unattended Houseplants* (McGough), describes a device which dispenses a quantity of water (typically 16 or 32 ounces) to a potted houseplant over an extended period of time (typically 1 to 2 weeks or more) without owner intervention. The bottle-type device is completely passive, operates by gravity flow, uses standard tap water, and solves a number of problems not addressed by earlier houseplant watering devices. The -700 device is comprised of three major components, one of which is a disk-shaped sandwich-type wafer constructed of several layers of gasket material, laboratory filter paper, and thin plastic, having through-holes and passages so constructed as to filter impurities from the water and control the rate at which water is released from the reservoir during the desired watering period. The -700 device dispenses the reservoir water over a specified time period, releases its water at a relatively uniform rate during the watering cycle, uses standard tap water, and is simple to manufacture and install. The -700 device has been on the market for several years and has proven to be an effective method for watering a wide variety of unattended houseplants.

(0006) Another device, called a *Tree Irrigator* (US Patent 5,117,582, Cissel, Jr. et. al) utilizes a large flexible plastic bag (typically 20-gallon capacity) which encircles the trunk of a small tree, and which contains small holes in its base to dispense water over a period of time (typically 6 to 8 hours) to the tree.

(0007) Other prior devices have been suggested for irrigating unattended plants, and a number of these have received US patents.

(0008) US Patent 5,443,544 (Azoulay) describes a device which uses a wick and water-absorbing sponge to transfer water to the plant.

(0009) US Patent 4,970,823 (Chen and Parkhurst) describes another wick-type system for dispensing water from a bottle reservoir to the soil.

(0010) US Patent 4,578,897 (Pazar and Petrick) describes a system for dispensing water to a water dish located below the plant.

(0011) US Patent 4,336,666 (Caso) describes a toroidal-shaped device which requires the operator to punch holes in the "metering nozzles" to obtain the desired flow rate.

(0012) US Patent 4,300,309 (Mincy) uses a "porous soil penetrating member" to dispense water from the semi-toroid shaped reservoir to the soil.

(0013) Similarly, US Patents 4,089,133 (Duncan); 2,387,869 (Chatten); 2,595,783 (Epstein); and 2,375,860 (Markham) attempt to solve the problem of watering plants with various wicking, porous ceramic absorption, or multiple aperture devices.

(0014) US Patent 5,259,142 (Sax) employs a simple filter to restrict the flow of water from a rigid bottle, but provides no means of preventing the filter from becoming clogged by impurities in the water, and no means of sealing its filter disk against peripheral leakage.

(0015) All of the above patents describe various methods for automatically dispensing water to growing plants. However, only the first patent cited (US 5,896,700) bears any similarity in design or operating principle to the device disclosed herein. The -700 device uses a multilayered disk made of layers of thin plastic, filter paper, and gasket to filter and regulate the slow drip of the water from a plastic bottle over an extended period of time (typically 1 to 2 weeks). In the -700 device the disk is compressed between the lip of a plastic bottle and a hard plastic spike which is threaded on to the bottle neck. The device described in this application uses a similar multilayered disk to dispense 3 to 4 quarts of water over 2 to 3 weeks, except such disk is designed to be used with a flexible biodegradable bag, rather than the rigid plastic bottle and cap used in the -700 device.

SUMMARY OF THE INVENTION
(0016) The device disclosed herein is a modification and new application of the invention covered by US Patent 5,896,700 described in the previous section. This biodegradable one-time-use device is designed to provide water to newly planted tree seedlings and other similar small plants to prevent them from drying out in the critical 2- to 3-week period after planting. The device is comprised of two main components: (1) a unique version of the flow-control wafer described in the -700 patent, herein called a drip-control disk; and (2) a biodegradable plastic bag made of cornstarch or other similar material, capable of holding, typically 1 gallon of water, having a sealable top opening for filling the water, and into which is permanently installed the drip-control disk. After the bag is filled with water it is placed near the base of the newly planted seedling or plant, with the drip-control disk downward, where it will slowly release its water over a specified time period (typically 2 to 3 weeks) to keep the plant roots moist. After the bag empties it will slowly degrade into the soil, typically over 40 to 45 days, so as to not leave debris in the forest or planting area.

BRIEF DESCRIPTION OF THE DRAWINGS

(0017) Figure 1 shows the biodegradable plastic bag (approximately 1 gallon capacity) with sealable top-filling opening and drip-control disk. The top-filling opening is shown in its open position. The sealing flap contains a layer of double-backed tape for sealing the flap to the bag.

(0018) Figure 2a and Figure 2b show the bag's double-back tape closure in its open and sealed positions.

(0019) Figure 3 shows details of the critical drip-control disk, which controls the rate at which water is slowly released from the bag into the soil surrounding the seedling or other small plant.

DETAILED DESCRIPTION OF THE INVENTION

(0020) A device for irrigating seedlings and other small plants, especially in the period immediately following planting, to ensure that the roots of said plantings remain moist, consists of a biodegradable plastic bag 1 having a typical capacity of 1 gallon of water, said bag having a sealable top opening 2 and, at the bottom, a multilayered drip-control disk 3 which controls the rate at which water is slowly released from the bag. In the preferred embodiment the sealable top opening has a double-back tape strip 4 which will enable the operator to quickly fill, close, and place the bag by the plant. Other type closures may also be used.

(0021) The drip-control disk will release the contents of the bag over the desired period, typically 3 quarts over 2 to 3 weeks. Alternatively, other capacities and release times may be used, depending on the specific needs of the plant.

(0022) Figure 1 is an overall view of the device showing the biodegradable plastic bag with sealable top-fill port and the drip-control disk near the bottom. The configuration of the bag shown is basically triangular, although other shapes, such as rectangular, can also be used as long as the sealable fill port is at or near the top of the bag.

(0023) The bag is thin-walled (typically 0.001 inch or less) and made of a material, such as plasticized cornstarch, which degrades into the soil when exposed to sunlight and moisture over a period of time, typically 40 to 45 days. Such bags are commonly used in many applications where environmental considerations are important.

(0024) The multilayered drip-control disk is located on or near the bottom of the bag, as shown in Figure 1, so that it can be placed very near to the base of the seedling or small plant to ensure that the water soaks the roots as it drips from the filled bag.

(0025) Also, as shown in Figure 1, the fill port of the bag has a closure flap upon which is attached a strip of double-back adhesive tape. After the bag is filled with water to the desired level, the operator removes the backing from the double-back tape and seals the closure flap to the bag, as shown in Figure 2a (open) 4 and Figure 2b (sealed) 5. Because this is a one-time-use product, the bag is not intended to be reopened and this simple inexpensive closure method can be used in lieu of more expensive reclosable systems.

(0026) Figure 3 shows details of the drip-control disk, as attached to the biodegradable plastic bag **1**. The disk consists of four layers: (1) A top layer of thin plastic sheet **6**, approximately 1 inch in diameter, said plastic having a layer of adhesive material on its lower surface; (2) a layer of special laboratory filter paper **7**, also approximately 1 inch in diameter; (3) a second layer of thin plastic sheet **8**, said layer having a layer of adhesive material on its top surface and a center hole **9** approximately one-quarter (1/4) inch in diameter; and (4) a rectangular or circular shaped layer of thin flexible gasket material **10** somewhat larger than the disk made up of layers 1, 2, and 3, and having adhesive on its top surface and a small hole **11**, approximately one-quarter (1/4) inch in diameter in its center.

(0027) Layers 1, 2, and 3 are assembled so that the adhesive layers of the two plastic sheets touch the filter paper and bond the three layers together into a single three-layer subassembly.

(0028) Said subassembly is then compressed in a hydraulic press by a predetermined amount as determined by testing, so that the adhesive is driven into the surfaces of the filter paper to create a flow-path resistance which will cause the installed drip-disk to release all of the water in the bag in the desired 2- to 3-week period.

(0029) The circle-shaped subassembly disk is then placed on the outside surface of the bag between 2 small holes **12**, each approximately one-quarter (1/4) inch in diameter, located near the bottom of the bag. Said small holes are separated by a distance equal to the diameter of the subassembly disk.

(0030) The open edges of the filter paper in the said subassembly disk thus intersect the 2 small holes in the bag. The thin gasket sheet is then placed over said subassembly disk, adhesive side up, so that the center holes of the subassembly disk and the flexible gasket sheet are concentric. The flexible gasket sheet is then pressed down firmly to seal the subassembly disk against the outer surface of the biodegradable plastic bag.

(0031) To irrigate seedlings and small plants, the operator fills the bag with water through its top-filling opening, removes the backing layer from the strip of double-back tape, folds said strip and presses it against the surface of the bag to seal the opening. The operator then places the filled bag next to the seedling or small plant, so that said drip-control disk is as close to the base of said seedling or small plant as practical.

(0031) The water from the bag then follows a flow path **13** as it passes slowly through the holes in the bag, then laterally through the compressed filter paper, down through the concentric center holes in the lower plastic and gasket sheets, and into the soil surrounding the roots of the seedling or small plant. The desired 2- to 3-week period in which the bag empties its full capacity is achieved through the design, manufacture, and testing of the said drip-control disks under actual operating conditions.

(0032) The specific size, shape, and materials of the bag, and the dimensions of the component parts, as described in the above paragraphs, are intended to illustrate the principles of this device, but said descriptions are not intended to restrict this invention to the specific details included herein.

Sample 9 — Continued

Note: The following is the claims section mentioned in section 1.2 of Chapter 8. This section should be completed by a patent attorney or patent agent.

CLAIMS

I claim:
(0033) 1. A device for irrigating tree seedlings and other small plants, which consists of: (1) a bag capable of containing water which is constructed of flexible, biodegradable plastic made of cornstarch or other similar material, said bag having a top-filling opening which can be sealed by means of a strip of double-back paper tape, and said bag having a hole or holes in its lower area; and (2) a multilayered disk consisting of two thin sheets of plastic, both said plastic sheets having one side coated with adhesive and one said plastic sheet containing a small center hole, and one sheet of laboratory filter paper, so that when the layers of said plastic sheets and filter paper are assembled and compressed together and then attached to said bag by a sheet of adhesive-sided gasket material, said gasket sheet being slightly larger in area than the plastic and filter paper sheets and also having a small center hole, so that the edge of said compressed assembly is located directly over said hole or holes in the lower area of said bag; so that said multilayered disk can control the passage of water from said bag into the plant soil at the desired slow rate as determined by testing.

(0034) 2. The device described in Claim 1., wherein the multilayered disk consists of two thin sheets of plastic, each said plastic sheet having one side coated with adhesive and one said plastic sheet containing a small center hole, and one sheet of laboratory filter paper, so that when the layers of said plastic sheets and filter paper are assembled and compressed together and then attached by a sheet of adhesive-sided gasket material, said gasket sheet being slightly larger in area than the plastic and filter paper sheets and also having a small center hole, so that the edge of said compressed assembly is located directly over said hole or holes in the lower area of said bag, so that said multilayered disk can control the passage of water from said bag into the plant soil at the desired slow rate as determined by testing.

(0035) 3. The device described in Claim 1., wherein the container holding the water is a bag constructed of flexible, biodegradable plastic made of cornstarch or other similar material, said bag having a top-filling opening which can be sealed by a strip of double-back paper tape, and a hole or holes in its lower area.

ABSTRACT
(0036) This invention is a device for irrigating tree seedlings and other small plants, to ensure that said plants stay moist in the critical few weeks following their planting. The device uses a bag, approximately 1 gallon capacity, constructed of biodegradable plastic, such as cornstarch, which slowly degrades into the soil so as to not leave residue in the planting field. The bag has a top-filling opening with an adhesive-sealing flap, and contains a multilayered disk which acts as a passive valve which permits the slow-drip release of water from the bag over a 2- to 3-week period following planting. The multilayered disk is made of two layers of thin plastic, a layer of special laboratory filter paper, and a layer of adhesive-sided gasket material which attaches said disk to said biodegradable bag. The design of the hole patterns in the layers of the disk, and the assembly and precise compression of said layers during manufacture, result in a device that produces the desired slow-release flow characteristics.

Biodegradable Device for Irrigating Seedlings and Other Small Plants
Charles B. McGough

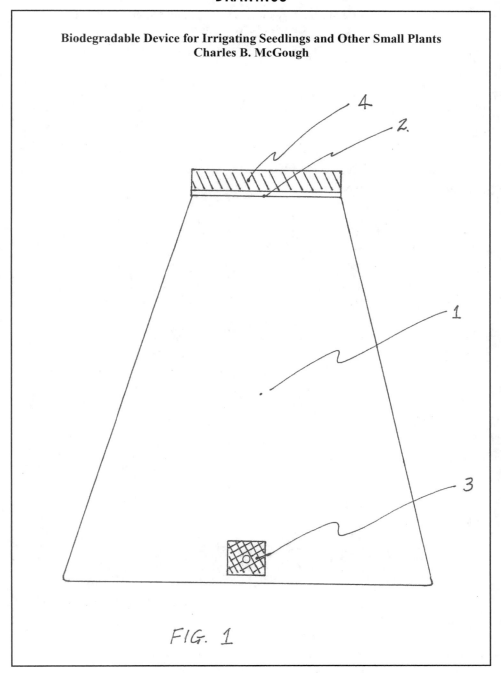

FIG. 1

Biodegradable Device for Irrigating Seedlings and Other Small Plants
Charles B. McGough

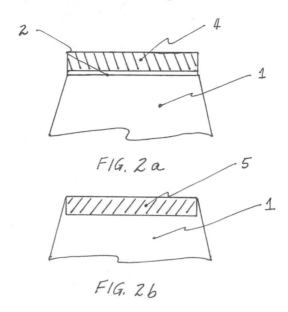

FIG. 2a

FIG. 2b

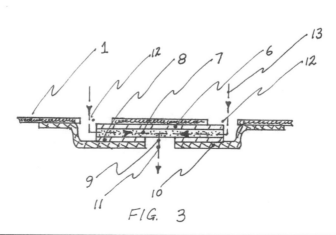

FIG. 3

11
Negotiate the License Agreement

You might wonder why you should attempt to license, rather than sell, your new product. The reason is simple: Most companies want to minimize the financial risk when they launch a new product. They know they will have to incur substantial costs to manufacture, package, advertise, distribute, and sell the product, and they will not want to risk any more than they have to for the product until they know they can successfully sell it. Nobody knows how well the product will sell, so the company will not want to purchase it outright before they know they can make a profit from it. What you want is the company to make the investment necessary to sell your product, so both you and the company will benefit.

The solution is a license agreement. This is the most common way new products are acquired by companies from independent inventors, which is why we will emphasize the licensing method in this chapter.

In a license agreement you (the licensor) will grant the company (the licensee) the right to make, use, and sell your invention (the product) in a specific region (the territory) for a specific period of time (the term). For this right, the licensee will pay the licensor (you) an agreed on amount of money (royalty) for the sale of each product unit.

It is recommended that you, as the inventor, reach an agreement with the interested company on the basic business terms of a license agreement. If you are experienced in business, you should be able to do this yourself without involving an attorney at this point. If you are not, you may feel more comfortable using a commercial attorney. To save money, you may not want to hire an attorney now unless absolutely necessary.

1. Prepare the Memorandum of Understanding

The Memorandum of Understanding (a business agreement) is not legally binding in itself, but will define the basic deal points to be included in a binding license agreement which will be drawn up and reviewed by lawyers on both sides.

The following bullet list discusses what should be included in the Memorandum of Understanding:

- **Parties defined:** This section defines the parties involved such as you, the licensor, and the company, the licensee. It also includes the addresses of both parties.

- **Product information:** This section defines the product, and states that all intellectual property, including patents and trademarks, both issued and pending, and all "know-how" are included in the license.

- **Territory:** This defines where the licensee may sell the product. This will probably be in the United States unless the licensee wants more territory (e.g., all of North America).

- **Type of agreement:** This means that you will not have the right to make or sell the product yourself or license it to others in this territory, but you will have the right to license and sell outside the territory.

- **Term:** This section covers the time limit of the agreement. For example, three years initial term, thereafter renewable annually by agreement of both parties.

- **Minimum sales requirement:** With the agreement of both parties this defines the minimum sales required of the licensee to keep the license. Keep this low for the first year to allow the licensee to get started, increasing as warranted by the type of product and the market.

- **Technical support:** You should agree to provide technical support to the licensee for a specific period (e.g., one year) at no cost to the licensee except for reimbursement of your out-of-pocket expenses. This is especially important if your product is technical in nature. I know of one instance where the inventor traveled to China, at the licensee's request, to train the licensee's manufacturer, and several other cases where the inventor supported the licensee sales teams in key presentations to important customers and at trade shows. Obviously, it is in your own best interest to help the licensee make the product successful.

- **Review of artwork:** The inventor must have the right to review and comment on all packaging, display, and advertising artwork before it is finalized. The licensee will have the final say, but it has been shown many times that embarrassing and expensive errors in text and drawings could have been avoided had the inventor been able to review this material before final printing.

- **Markings:** Your licensee's product should always include the statement "Manufactured and distributed by *(name of licensee company)* under license from *(name and city of licensor)*." Also, it should give the numbers of all applicable issued patents. This information should be placed on all packaging and advertising.

- **Royalty:** The royalty is typically eight to ten percent of the licensee's (not the retailer's) revenues from the sale of the product. Royalties are normally paid quarterly, accompanied by a report of units sold. There are a number of ways of calculating this payment, but the simplest is to agree on a flat dollar amount to be paid per unit sold.

- **License fee:** It is common for the licensor to receive an upfront payment from the licensee on signing of the license. The amount will depend on the product itself and the licensee's expected sales.

Be reasonable in the up-front fee you request. One suggestion is 50 percent of the royalties from the licensee's first-year sales forecast. It is important to sign a good company that will promote the product and pay you regular royalties over the life of the patent, and you do not want to jeopardize this by haggling over the up-front fee.

If the company balks at paying a flat up-front license fee, then suggest that it be in the form of a nonrefundable advance royalty payment. This gives you some up-front money which the company can credit against future earned royalties. It is very important that the licensee have some "skin in the game" so that he or she will not simply sign the agreement, sit on it, and do little or nothing to promote and sell the product.

- **Termination provisions:** This section should allow the licensor to terminate the agreement if the licensee fails to achieve the agreed-on quarterly sales and royalties.

- **Exclusivity period:** The inventor and the company should agree to work exclusively with each other, and in confidence, to arrive at a mutually acceptable license agreement within a specific period of time. This period is typically two to three months, maximum. If that time expires without a signed license agreement, the inventor is free to negotiate with others.

- **Signing the document:** The Memorandum of Understanding must be signed and dated by you, the inventor and licensor, and by an authorized officer of the licensee company.

The legally binding license agreement itself must be prepared and/or reviewed by business (not patent) attorneys. Because the licensing company will probably have its own in-house or outside attorneys, and most likely will have done this many times, you may want to let the licensing company draft the agreement. This will save you the expense of doing this. You can then have your business attorney review this draft and negotiate with the company lawyer any changes to the boilerplate needed to protect your interests. However, there should be no changes made to the basic deal points of the Memorandum of Understanding without your approval.

12
Don't Relax after Signing the Agreement

You have now accomplished some very important goals. You have invented and tested a promising new product. You have registered your provisional patent application and applied for the critical non-provisional patent application which will protect your idea for 20 years when issued. You have come up with a great name and trademarked it. You have found a company to manufacture and sell your product, and you negotiated and signed your license agreement.

Those are major accomplishments of which you can be proud, but you're not quite finished. In order to get the most out of your great idea, you should consider the additional tasks described in this chapter.

1. You're Not Done Yet!

The following sections discuss a few things you can do after your license agreement is signed. There may be many others as well, depending on your idea. Don't rest on your laurels, but keep moving forward!

The old ballplayer Satchel Paige once advised, "Don't look back. Something might be gaining on you." I advise inventors to do the opposite. Keep a good eye on the competition, keep improving your product, support your valued licensee, and look for new ideas, so that somebody does *not* gain on you!

1.1 Improve your product

Continue to test and improve your product even after the license agreement has been signed. You should not assume that your current design is necessarily the best version. Keep testing and improving it until you are confident that you have reached the point of diminishing value.

1.2 Monitor the competition

When a new product appears on the market that claims to perform a similar function, buy one and test it yourself. You will need this information to answer questions from your licensee and customers. You are expected to be an expert in your field, so keep on top of your competitors.

1.3 Support your licensee

Make sure that you tell your licensee about any product improvements you make, and what you have learned about your competitors. If the licensee requests, train his or her sales and manufacturing people, and support the licensee at trade shows. Agree to reasonable royalty discounts for special high-volume opportunities. Remember, if the licensee succeeds, you succeed.

1.4 Create more inventions

Consider creating spin-off inventions. You may find that your product inspires other ideas that you could turn into new patents and new licenses.

1.5 Avoid scams

Once your patent issues, your mailbox will be inundated with offers from many companies praising your idea and offering to promote and sell it for you. They will ask for a substantial upfront payment, periodic payments, and often a slice of your future royalties. Ignore them all. There is nothing that they can do for you that you can't do better yourself. Remember, you know more about your product than anyone, and you have the guidance of this book to help you sell it effectively!

Conclusion
Congratulations for a Job Well Done!

You have traveled a long and, hopefully rewarding, inventor's yellow brick road to success. First, you came up with your idea for a great new product. You gave your idea a tough-love evaluation; made and tested a working model; estimated its manufacturing costs; protected it for one year with a Provisional Application for Patent; trademarked a cool name for your product; found at least one good company to license it; filed your nonprovisional patent application to protect it for 20 more years; negotiated and signed a fair license agreement with a licensee company; and you are now continuing to follow up on your good work. If you have completed all, or at least most, of the tasks in this book you can be really proud of your accomplishments! For an example of an approved patent, see Sample 11.

I hope that your product will soon join the ranks of other great ideas. The milk carton that changes color to indicate the milk's freshness; a clever new restaurant chair which protects a woman's handbag from purse snatchers; a unique compact wall plug that replaces clumsy power strips; or a neat little device to help people with limited mobility write and hold small tools. The list is endless.

One of my favorite success stories, which has received a lot of press recently, is about a body-shaping hosiery called Spanx. The inventor, Sara Blakely, was 27 years old when she came up with an idea to eliminate the feet on pantyhose and remove visible panty lines under her close-fitting garments. She wrote her own patent and negotiated a discount with a patent attorney to file for her patent. Today, Spanx and its sister products are sold in 10,000 retail stores producing $350 million per year in sales revenues. What an inspiring story!

Your product may or may not be this successful, but if you follow the path laid out in this book, you will know that you gave it your best shot.

Here's one final story for you: Patrick Garner from New Jersey makes his living impersonating Thomas Edison. When asked why he does this he replied, "My biggest reward is when a kid says, 'I want to grow up to be an inventor!'"

Good luck, and keep your great inventions coming!

The Commissioner of Patents and Trademarks

Has received an application for a patent for a new and useful invention. The title and description of the invention are enclosed. The requirements of law have been complied with, and it has been determined that a patent on the invention shall be granted under the law.

Therefore, this

United States Patent

Grants to the person(s) having title to this patent the right to exclude others from making, using, offering for sale, or selling the invention throughout the United States of America or importing the invention into the United States of America for the term set forth below, subject to the payment of maintenance fees as provided by law.

If this application was filed prior to June 8, 1995, the term of this patent is the longer of seventeen years from the date of grant of this patent or twenty years from the earliest effective U.S. filing date of the application, subject to any statutory extension.

If this application was filed on or after June 8, 1995, the term of this patent is twenty years from the U.S. filing date, subject to any statutory extension. If the application contains a specific reference to an earlier filed application or applications under 35 U.S.C. 120, 121 or 365(c), the term of the patent is twenty years from the date on which the earliest application was filed, subject to any statutory extension.

Acting Commissioner of Patents and Trademarks

NOTICE

If the application for this patent was filed on or after December 12, 1980, maintenance fees are due three years and six months, seven years and six months, and eleven years and six months after the date of this grant, or within a grace period of six months thereafter upon payment of a surcharge as provided by law. The amount, number and timing of the maintenance fees required may be changed by law or regulation. Unless payment of the applicable maintenance fee is received in the Patent and Trademark Office on or before the date the fee is due or within a grace period of six months thereafter, the patent will expire as of the end of such grace period.

US005896700A

United States Patent [19]

McGough

[11] Patent Number:	**5,896,700**
[45] Date of Patent:	**Apr. 27, 1999**

[54] **DEVICE FOR WATERING UNATTENDED HOUSEPLANTS**

[76] Inventor: **Charles B. McGough**, 27 Deepwells La., St. James, N.Y. 11780

[21] Appl. No.: **08/731,018**

[22] Filed: **Oct. 9, 1996**

[51] Int. Cl.[6] A01G 29/00
[52] U.S. Cl. 47/48.5
[58] Field of Search 47/48.5, 1.01

[56] **References Cited**

U.S. PATENT DOCUMENTS

2,791,347	5/1957	Boehm	47/48.5
4,785,575	11/1988	Shioi	47/48.5
4,970,823	11/1990	Chen et al.	47/48.5
5,172,515	12/1992	Lapshansky, Sr. et al.	47/48.5
5,259,142	11/1993	Sax	47/48.5
5,443,544	8/1995	Azoulay	47/48.5

FOREIGN PATENT DOCUMENTS

1217816	5/1960	France	47/48.5
1151974	7/1963	Germany	47/48.5

Primary Examiner—Michael J. Carone
Assistant Examiner—Joanne C. Downs

[57] **ABSTRACT**

This invention is a device for automatically watering unattended houseplants with ordinary tap water. The device controls the rate of discharge of water from a reservoir by means of a replaceable multilayer sandwich-type flow control wafer, which is made of several layers of deformable gasket material, laboratory filtration paper, and thin flexible plastic. The gasket and plastic layers contain designed patterns of through-holes and passages which force the water to flow over and through the filtration paper to control the rate of release of water from the reservoir. The design also uses the filtration paper to remove particles from the tap water which could clog the system and stop the flow. Over the course of the watering cycle the water gradually loosens the adhesive bonds between the filtration paper and the plastic, which increases the effective flow area of the filtration paper to partially compensate for the reduction in pressure head which occurs as the reservoir empties, thus keeping the water flow rate more constant over the watering cycle than it would be if controlled only by a simple orifice or filter. The watering device includes registration and compression rings which position and seal the flow control wafer, a concave funnel-like reservoir opening for filling the device in situ, and a narrow integral spike which supports the device in the plant soil and creates an open vertical passage which facilitates water penetration deep into the plant's root system.

6 Claims, 4 Drawing Sheets

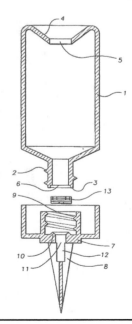

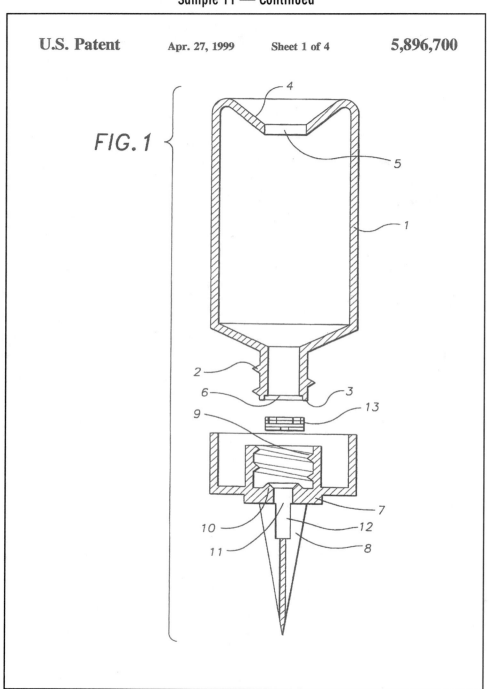

U.S. Patent   Apr. 27, 1999   Sheet 1 of 4   5,896,700

FIG. 1

U.S. Patent   **Apr. 27, 1999**   **Sheet 2 of 4**   **5,896,700**

FIG.2a

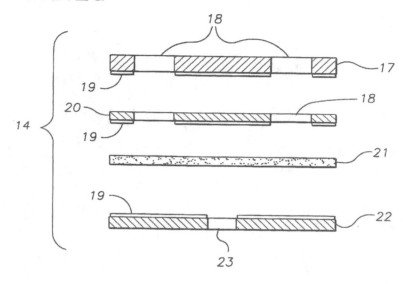

FIG.2b

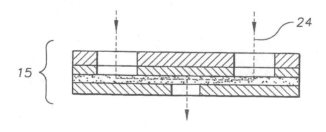

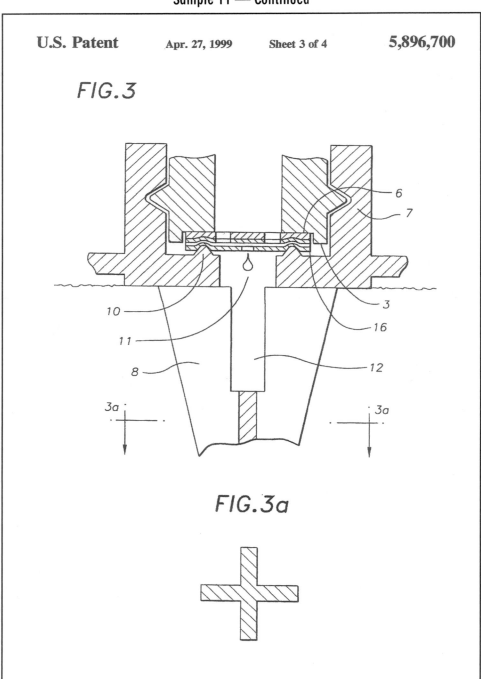

U.S. Patent   Apr. 27, 1999   Sheet 4 of 4   5,896,700

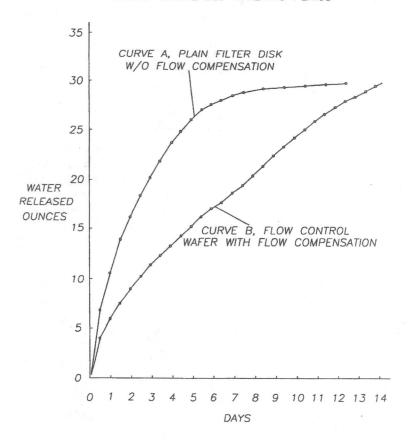

FIG.4

CUMULATIVE WATER RELEASED FROM RESERVOIR
DURING UNATTENDED WATERING PERIOD

5,896,700

3

volume to provide water to the plant for approximately two weeks. It has been found that a 32 ounce reservoir is suitable for plants contained in 10 inch diameter pots or larger, and a 16 ounce reservoir is suitable for smaller plants. This invention is not intended to be limited to these specific sizes. More than one watering device may be used for very large plants or indoor trees. The reservoir contains a male threaded exit neck 2 having an opening smaller than the reservoir diameter, with a smooth, flat lower surface 3 suitable for sealing. It has been found that a 0.8125-inch inside diameter neck works well for this device, although other neck diameters may also be used. The top of the reservoir contains a funnel-like concave-shaped depression 4 with a hole at its base 5 so that the device may be easily filled in situ after installation in the plant, using a standard watering can. The top opening also provides venting so that atmospheric pressure is maintained in the reservoir as it empties.

The reservoir exit neck lower surface includes a low (e.g. 0.040 inch) raised outer registration ridge 6 so that the flow control wafer can be easily placed in its correct position by the operator during installation. This registration ridge shall be slightly greater in diameter than the cap compression ring (see below) to prevent interference with the sealing.

Base Assembly: The base assembly 7 serves five major functions: (1) It supports the device by means of a narrow tapered spike 8 having a cruciform-shaped cross section, inserted into the plant soil, (2) It contains a matching female threaded joint 9 used to attach the base assembly to the male threaded exit neck of the reservoir, (3) It contains a raised compression ring 10 at the base of the threads, which is slightly larger in diameter than the inside diameter of the reservoir neck. This compression ring tightly compresses the flow control wafer (described below) against the lower flat surface of the reservoir exit neck 3 to prevent water leakage, (4) It provides a small outlet plenum 11 with a bottom opening to allow free passage of the water into said support spike, (5) It provides, by means of an open center section in the upper region of said support spike 12, a vertical passage in the soil which facilitates water flow to below the soil surface to minimize evaporation and to allow the water to penetrate more easily into the plant root system.

Flow Control Wafer: The replaceable flow control wafer 13 is a key element of this invention. The flow control wafer is a circular-shaped multilayered disk, typically 1 inch in diameter and 0.055 inch or less in thickness. It is shown in exploded view 14, assembled 15, and tightly sealed between the reservoir exit neck and the base assembly by the compression ring 16 . The functions of the various layers of the flow control wafer are:

1. Layer 1 is a deformable material (e.g. rubber or soft plastic) disk or O-ring approximately 1.0 inch in diameter 17. It serves as a gasket which creates a seal between the reservoir exit neck and the flow control wafer to prevent circumferential leakage from the reservoir. The Layer 1 disk or O-ring contains one or more through-holes or passages 18 which allow free passage of water from the reservoir to the layer below. Layer 1 may or may not have adhesive 19 on its lower surface to bond it to Layer 2.

2. Layer 2 is a smooth, flexible plastic disk 20 with adhesive on its lower surface 19. This disk is approximately 0.005 inches thick and has through-holes directly below the through-holes or passages of Layer 1.

3. Layer 3 is a disk made from one or more layers of laboratory grade filtration paper 21. The specific paper

4

type has been selected through testing to filter impurities from the water and to provide a relatively uniform flowrate for a specified watering cycle with the desired reservoir capacity (typically 32 or 16 ounces). If more than one layer of filtration paper is used, a layer of thin plastic, smaller in diameter than the filtration paper disks, may be inserted between the paper layers to create a more labyrinthine water flow path.

4. Layer 4 is a smooth, flexible plastic disk approximately 0.005 inches thick 22 with adhesive on its upper surface 20. This disk also contains one or more through-holes which may or may not be aligned with the hole pattern of Layer 2. Layer 4 is bonded to the lower surface of the Layer 3 filtration paper by means of adhesive on its top surface.

After bonding, the assembly comprising Layers 1, 2, 3, and 4 is compressed to remove entrapped air. The completed flow control wafer is a rugged, one-piece, semi-flexible, replaceable disk.

The sandwich configuration of the flow control wafer in which one or more layers of laboratory filtration paper is bonded between two or more thin disks having various hole patterns, forces the water to enter the top hole pattern and flow vertically and horizontally through and over the paper to reach the exit hole or holes in the lower plastic disk 24. At the beginning of the cycle, when the reservoir is full and the hydraulic pressure on the filtration paper is highest, the flowrate would be excessively high if allowed to pass directly through the paper without being forced to follow the labyrinthine path of the multilayer flow control wafer. This restricted path initially reduces the equivalent "frontal area" available to the water as it passes from the reservoir, through the filtration paper, and into the base assembly. However, as the water saturates the filtration paper it gradually loosens the adhesive which bonds the paper to the plastic layers. Therefore, two partially compensating effects are occurring simultaneously; (1) the hydraulic pressure above the flow control wafer is decreasing as the water level in the bottle drops, and (2) the filtration paper frontal area is increasing and the effective distance through which the flow passes is decreasing as the paper-to-plastic bonds are loosened by the water. This effect, herein termed "flow compensation", enables the watering device to deliver a more constant flow of water to the plant over time than can be achieved by a simple gravity flow device.

The flow compensation effect can be understood by examining Poiseuille's equation(1), which governs the laminar flow of a liquid through a porous medium,

$$F = KPA/L$$

where, in any compatible units,

F=flowrate through the filter

P=hydraulic static pressure on the filter

A=effective frontal filter area

L=distance through which fluid flows through the medium

K=filter medium permeability constant

1. Brown, George G. and Associates, Unit Operations, (New York, John Wiley & Sons, 1955, p. 217.

This equation shows that an increase in the flow area, A, and/or a decrease in the flow path length, L, will tend to partially compensate for the decrease in the pressure head, P, which occurs as the reservoir empties, thus keeping the flowrate, F, more nearly constant.

The flow compensation effect has been demonstrated in tests performed by the inventor. FIG. 4 shows the cumulative volume of water discharged in a typical test from a 30

Sample 11 — Continued

5,896,700

5

ounce reservoir over a fourteen day period, using both a flow control wafer with flow compensation and a plain filter without flow compensation. As can be seen from these data, the simple filter system without flow compensation (Curve A) discharged the water rapidly, consuming 80% of the water (24 ounces) in the first four days, with only 20% (6 ounces) available to the plant in the remaining ten days of the cycle. The flow control wafer with flow compensation (Curve B), however, restricted the flow path early in the cycle and dispensed more water later in the watering period when it is most needed by the plant. The data from these tests show that at the same four day point where the non-compensated filter disk used 80% of the water, the compensated flow control wafer used only 43%, conserving 57%, or 17 ounces, for the remaining ten days of the cycle.

Many variations in detail may be made to the preferred embodiment described above without altering the basic principles of the invention. These include: the filtration paper manufacturer, model, thickness, and/or permeability; the number, size, and location of through-holes and passages in the flow control wafer; the deformable gasket material and configuration (e.g. rubber, vinyl, soft plastic materials; disk or O-ring configuration); the diameters of the reservoir neck opening and flow control wafer; the reservoir and base assembly materials of construction; support spike configurations, including circular and other cross-sections, various lengths, and other similar variations thereof.

The preferred embodiment, and all variations thereof, are manufactured entirely of standard, low-cost, commercially available materials, and require very little labor. The device can therefore be produced at low cost which will make it practical to manufacture and distribute to the consumer market.

What is claimed is:

1. A device for automatically watering unattended houseplants, said device comprising a water reservoir having a bottom threaded exit neck with a flat lower surface, and a top filling and venting opening; a base assembly constructed of hard plastic and having a threaded joint which mates to said bottom threaded exit neck of said water reservoir, and having a bottom opening through which water can pass into an upper section of a narrow tapered spike which supports said houseplant watering device and allows passage of water into the soil of a houseplant; and a replaceable disk-shaped flow control wafer, which is retained between said exit neck of said water reservoir and said threaded joint of said base assembly, said flow control wafer comprising a top layer of deformable gasket material having one or more through-holes; a second layer located directly below said top layer, said second layer consisting of a sheet of thin plastic material having a pattern of one or more through-holes; a third layer located directly below said second layer, said third layer consisting of one or more sheets of filtration paper having no through-holes, in which said sheets of filtration paper may or may not be separated by a thin layer of plastic material having no through-holes and having a diameter slightly smaller than the diameter of said one or more sheets of filtration paper; and a fourth layer located directly below said third layer, said fourth layer consisting of a sheet of thin plastic material having one or more through-holes; so that the arrangement of said layers of gasket material, filtration paper, and plastic sheets forces the water to follow a predetermined labyrinthine path as it flows

6

from said water reservoir into said base assembly; so that said water reservoir, base assembly, and flow control wafer, when assembled together, comprise a leak-tight, compact device capable of dispensing water to a houseplant over a predefined period of time.

2. The device described in claim 1 wherein said one or more sheets of filtration paper are commercially-available laboratory filtration paper having the same or different porosities, with said porosities selected to provide a water release rate consistent with an intended watering period for said houseplant, and to remove impurities in the water which would clog said watering device and impede the flow of water to the houseplant.

3. The device described in claim 1 wherein said flow control wafer is comprised of layers of said deformable gasket material, said sheets of filtration paper, and said sheets of thin plastic material, with said gasket and plastic layers having said patterns of through-holes, and said sheets of filtration paper having no through-holes, so that, when said layers of deformable gasket material, filtration paper, and thin plastic are bonded by adhesives to one another in a sandwich configuration to form a single integrated wafer, said wafer filters the water and forces the water to flow through the wafer in a predetermined path, which path becomes less restrictive as the adhesives are gradually unbonded by the dissolving action of the water, which unbonding partially compensates for a reduction of pressure head as said water reservoir gradually empties, which enables said houseplant watering device to release the water to the houseplant at a relatively uniform rate.

4. The device described in claim 1 wherein said base assembly contains a sealing system consisting of a circular narrow raised ridge located directly below said flat lower surface of said reservoir exit neck, so that said raised ridge tightly compresses said flow control wafer against said flat lower surface of said exit neck of said water reservoir to prevent peripheral leakage of water into said threaded joint between said reservoir exit neck and said base assembly, thus ensuring that all water passes through said flow control wafer.

5. The device described in claim 1 wherein said flow control wafer is held in position directly below said water reservoir exit neck by means of a positioning and retaining system consisting of said reservoir exit neck having said flat lower surface made with a shallow raised outer ridge, said raised outer ridge being slightly larger in diameter than said flow control wafer, so that easy and accurate positioning and retention of said flow control wafer can be achieved during threading of said water reservoir to said base assembly of said houseplant watering device.

6. The device described in claim 1 wherein said narrow tapered spike contains a hollow vertical center section in an upper region thereof with horizontal side openings, so that, when said narrow tapered spike is inserted fully into the soil of a houseplant to support said houseplant watering device, said hollow vertical center section creates a vertical path in the houseplant soil equal to the length of said hollow vertical center section of said narrow tapered spike, which allows water to pass directly from said flow control wafer down said hollow vertical center section of said narrow tapered spike and directly into the root system of a houseplant.

* * * * *

Download Kit

Please enter the URL you see in the box below into your computer web browser to access and download the kit.

www.self-counsel.com/updates/invention/14forms.htm

The kit includes forms in PDF and MS Word formats so that you can print them out and edit them to meet your needs:

- Provisional Application for Patent
- Specification (Provisional Patent Application)
- Certification of Micro Entity Status
- Utility Patent Application
- Fee Transmittal
- Declaration for Utility or Design Patent Application
- Specification (Nonprovisional Patent Application)
- Resources